Still
the
Trumpet
Sounds

Books by J. Wallace Hamilton

HORNS AND HALOS IN HUMAN NATURE

RIDE THE WILD HORSES!

WHO GOES THERE?

SERENDIPITY

THE THUNDER OF BARE FEET

WHERE NOW IS THY GOD?

STILL THE TRUMPET SOUNDS

J. Wallace Hamilton

STILL
THE
TRUMPET
SOUNDS

Fleming H. Revell Company
Old Tappan, New Jersey

Scripture quotations identified KJV are from the *King James Version of the Bible*.

Scripture quotations identified RSV are from the *Revised Standard Version of the Bible*, Copyrighted 1946 and 1952.

Grateful acknowledgment is extended for the work of the following authors.

Edna St. Vincent Millay. *Conversation at Midnight*, Harper and Row. Copyright 1937 and 1964 by Edna St. Vincent Millay and Norma Millay Ellis.

Lines from "A Cockeyed Optimist," Copyright © 1949 by Richard Rodgers and Oscar Hammerstein II. Reprinted by permission of Williamson Music, Inc.

Lines from Tennessee Williams, *Sweet Bird of Youth*. Copyright © 1959 by Two Rivers Enterprises, Inc.

From the book *The Torchbearers*: "Watchers of the Sky" by Alfred Noyes. Copyright, 1922, by J. B. Lippincott Company. Renewal, 1950, by Alfred Noyes. Reprinted by permission of the publishers.

Diligent effort has been made to secure permission for the inclusion of all copyrighted material in this book. If any acknowledgments have been omitted, the publishers would appreciate receiving full information so that proper credit may be given in future editions.

To

*The men and women of
the Administrative Board of
Pasadena Community Church,
who through nearly forty years
believed in and encouraged
Dr. Hamilton in his ministry,
both in his own church and
in his preaching ministry
across the nation.*

Acknowledgment

When Dr. Hamilton died, he left six books of sermons published by Fleming H. Revell Company; each was made up of a series of sermons built around a central theme or idea. He also left a number of sermons marked, "Ready except for closer editing." Through the following winter I read these sermons and listened to recordings of them. (He dictated them from a handwritten copy every Sunday afternoon.) I did this to correct any small errors but more to be certain of his meaning before any editing was done on them. They represent a cross section of his preaching, on various themes and subjects, and from these I have selected the sermons in this book.

I wish to express here my gratitude to those who have helped me: to my sister Mrs. F. Ivan Burry and to Dr. Hamilton's sister Mrs. Stanley Hunt, for their constructive comments; to Miss Margaret E. Babbage who assisted me in the preliminary editing; to Mrs. Charles N. Osborne and Miss Merrily E. Taylor who typed the manuscript, their memorial to Dr. Hamilton; and to Bishop James W. Henley for his encouragement and support. And finally to Dr. Frank S. Mead for his editing and for his introductory "Appreciation" of Dr. Hamilton. Theirs was a rare friendship, like a bright flame, close and intimate. No other man is so qualified to write this, for Dr. Mead knew him as a man, a friend, a preacher and an author.

FLORENCE HAMILTON

The Golden Door

*. . . an appreciation of
a man and his preaching.*

IT SHOULD BE required of all preachers before they preach
that they make pilgrimage to the Statue of Liberty and
read there and memorize the words inscribed upon its
base:

I lift my lamp beside the golden door.

For this, you see, is true not only of the lady who holds
her torch above Manhattan's harbor, but even more of the
man called of God to hold high His lamp of faith and
hope and glory at the door of the Kingdom of Heaven. If
his preaching be weak and unworthy the light will be
uncertain, and few will find the door or enter in, but if
the light be bright and clear they will come from the ends
of the earth.

For more than forty years J. Wallace Hamilton lifted
such a lamp. Tens of thousands came to his Pasadena
Community Church in St. Petersburg, Florida, to hear
him, and multitudes more beat paths to other churches
in which he preached as he traveled up and down the

7

land. He opened the Kingdom door for them that they might look in and see, and what they saw was unbelievably beautiful.

Charles Clayton Morrison called him one of the six topmost representatives of the American pulpit. Norman Vincent Peale said that he was "one of the greatest preachers who ever gave expression to the Gospel in this country . . . I do not know that he had any peers at all." A host of laymen heard from him the finest sermons they ever heard and for every preacher he was a challenge to excellence.

There was a peculiar power in his sermons that both humbled and inspired. One Sunday morning, just before he left us, we went to hear him in the company of a lady who accompanied us with little enthusiasm and less expectancy. To put it quickly, she was fed up with preaching. She'd *had* it. She was angry with the preacher in her church at home, who, every Sunday morning at 11:35, preached furiously on racism, black suffering and white guilt. Given a text anywhere between Noah riding out the flood and John on Patmos, he got around eventually to race and the ghettos and the riots, and he lashed his captive congregation as the cause of it all. Our lady was weary of it. She'd had enough.

Hamilton preached that morning on Sapphira. Now we knew all about Sapphira—or thought we did—but we really didn't have much interest in her, especially as the subject of a sermon, and we wondered what he could do with her. It turned out that he knew Sapphira better than we did. He was always preaching on such obscure people, always picking up diamonds in the most unexpected places and polishing them, homiletically. Sapphira, he said, was as worthy of consideration as were Moses or Martha. Sapphira, wife of the liar Ananias, wasn't a *bad* woman, at least not as her husband was bad. She didn't steal anything, as he did; she knew what he was doing; she was privy to it, *but she did nothing about it.* She just went along with something she knew to be wrong. Not bad, not good; she just kept quiet about it. In one short, stabbing reference, Hamilton related her to the Christians who just go along with the race problem—the "good" people who say nothing and do nothing about an evil they know is so terribly wrong. At that moment there was a painful silence in the congregation; we were all looking at ourselves.

As we came out of the church, our lady—miracle of miracles!—was strangely silent.

"Well," we asked, "what did you think of *that*?"

With a glint of tears in her eyes she said, "He makes me so ashamed of what I have not done."

Actually, he was saying what the preacher back home had been saying—but with what a difference! The one infuriated her; the other inspired her. He opened doors.

This is power. Preaching power. He was somehow "different" among the preachers we have known. As a man, physically, he was shorter than most; he stood five feet six. But with that lamp in his hand, he was a giant.

The question that intrigues us about him is this: *How did he get that way*? Did he have some homiletic secret that eludes the rest of us? Was he just lucky in circumstances? Was he just, as so many have told us, a natural-born preacher? What made him so good and great in the pulpit?

Only yesterday we sat at luncheon with Bishop Gerald Kennedy of the United Methodist Church—a great preacher in his own right and one who heard and loved the preaching of his friend "Ham." The purpose of the luncheon was to talk about Ham and find out, if we could, what made him tick. To that end we asked a question.

"How do you account for it? Here was a boy who came off a hard-scrabble Canadian farm, who never went to college or theological seminary (he had only three years of schooling at Moody Bible Institute, by way of higher education), started preaching in a wide spot in the road called Baileyton, Tennessee, then came to a church in St. Petersburg that was dead and didn't know it. (Membership, 46; average congregation, 34; first Sunday's collection, $5.75.) When he died he had seen it grow into one of the finest churches in the United States. (Membership 3500; average congregation anywhere from 2500 to 10,000.) He was recognized as one of the finest preaching voices of our time. How come? What did it?"

The Bishop is a man of few and well-chosen words. "What did it?" he repeated. *Hard work did it*. Sure; he was born with a talent; so is every last one of us. But he didn't bury that talent. He worked at it day and night. He was never satisfied with his use of it; he was forever trying to *improve* it, if you know what I mean. First of all and beyond everything else, it was hard work!" He said much more, but those two words wrapped it up, neatly. In our hearts we shouted, "Amen!" and we thought of the

10

remark of Halford E. Luccock, who told a conference of preachers arguing bitterly about changes in the ritual of their church that it wasn't liturgy that was the trouble with most preachers; it was lethargy.

Hard work—hard, gruelling, endless work lay behind every sermon he ever preached. On Sunday afternoons, after the sermon of the morning, he began planning the sermon for next Sunday morning. This was *planning*, not the beginning. The start had been made weeks, months, even years before this: "When I get an idea," he said, "I make a folder for it and either put a Scripture passage in with it, or find one later. Then as I find material for it, I put it all in the folder. I am a good 'clipper-outer.' Any relevant thought that comes to me I write out and file. I do this so that when the time comes to prepare the sermon, I'll have something to begin with."

His study was a forest of folders, files, clippings and scrawled memos of ideas he had picked up at a Kiwanis luncheon or on the street or from a book or a child or a research scientist—illustrations clipped from magazines or marked in books, "Texts I Should Preach on," etc., ad infinitum. Most of it was filed, but there were stacks of it piled on desk, tables, chairs and bookcases. It was a labyrinth in which a stranger might easily get lost.

One file bulged with folders containing only sermon *Topics*. "Sometimes I keep folders for several years before I get around to developing them." In his book of sermons on *Serendipity*, he had material on that subject collected over a period of twenty-seven years. Fifteen sermons, one book—and twenty-seven years!

A second file held small cards under the general head-ing of *Subjects*. He explained, "When I find a good poem or quotation (for example, on the subject of courage), I write the reference down in longhand with the title of the book, the author and the page." Every book on his shelves was marked; there were magazines running the gamut from *The Pentecostal Holiness Advocate* to *Sports Illustrated*.

On Monday morning the hard work began. Five days a week, beginning with Monday, he was in his study from early morning to 1:00 P.M., and nothing short of an emergency was allowed to interrupt him. "The moment I sit down at my desk, I have a long-practiced ritual of listening. Revelation and guidance come hard to me. . . ." Just listening. Surrounded by this mountain of references, he sat and listened. Then, "I start writing. I put down whatever comes into my mind, however scrappy it may be. I develop an outline as quickly as I can, and keep writing for at least three mornings a week." On Saturday he put it on a tape recorder, played it back and listened carefully, making notes on a pad indicating changes that should be made. He heard himself preach the sermon before he went into the pulpit. Often, then, he rewrote the whole thing!

He wrote out every sermon, word for word. "When you write it out, you can phrase and rephrase ideas and keep them fresh and lively. Once I have made a path through the underbrush of an idea, it takes away any fear I might have when I stand in the pulpit to say it. I can leave the manuscript at home and feel confident that I can make my way through it." He never took either notes or manuscript into the pulpit; all he had there, in writing, were the quotations he would use, "so that I may use them accurately and give proper credit."

He had a strong conviction that the preacher was obligated, not only to tell the Good News, but to tell it "well, clearly and vitally." He said that a sermon should sing: "If in any part of a sermon you have a word that doesn't sing, then find one that does. . . . It is a frightening thing to see how dull and tame we have made the words of Christ. . . . We must make them live. No word has meaning until it comes alive, and every effort you make to find the right word, the right thing, brings you head-on into the divine imperative which is the Incarnation—the Word made flesh. This is the pain of preaching. None of us has the words, yet, to adequately convey the Word . . . we must find the word for it; we must wrestle with the words, must sit down with our heads in our hands. . . ."

Just *born* a great preacher? No. Preaching was anything but easy to him; it was an agony before it was an ecstacy. His startling language was born in sweat and struggle, and he always thought there was a better word beyond the one he used. Once he said to his editor, "You know, I should rewrite *Ride the Wild Horses* [his first book]; I think I could do a lot better with it now. . . ." That book, by that time, had been selling all across the country for sixteen years. On that same book, we had sat with him for thirty-five minutes trying to find exactly the right words for just one page of the manuscript.

He said, "I have to think hard." Dr. Morrison tells of attending a service in the Pasadena Church, expecting to hear a sermon on "The Greatness and Misery of Man," as the bulletin for the day promised. As Hamilton rose to

13

read the Scripture for the service and the sermon, he announced with apology that this sermon required more thinking on his part than he had been able to give it, so he would preach on another subject.

Preachers, seminary professors and students came from all points of the compass to hear and analyze his sermons. They came with little academic measuring sticks that were never adequate. We can no more capture the beauty of a sermon by tearing it apart than we can analyze the beauty of a rose by tearing its petals apart. We do not trap the Spirit in our little test tubes, and his sermons were Spirit-born and Spirit-guided. He was no mechanic following a blueprint issued from headquarters. In a way, he resembled the Billy Sunday who said, "If the English language gets in my way when I want to say something, it's just too bad for the English language." Hamilton was never guilty of murdering the king's English, but neither was he slave to any homiletic rule-of-thumb.

He had excellent construction in his sermons, though it was often so well hidden that his hearers missed it. If he had but one point to make, he made it and stopped. If he had two, or three points, he made them and sat down. At times he used the ancient and orthodox Introduction-Points-1-2-3-Conclusion formula; sometimes he did not. He didn't always say it according to the book, but he always said it well.

What makes a good preacher? Hard work, orderly construction and concentration. Wallace Hamilton knew early in his career what he wanted to do—preach! He stood for almost forty years in the pulpit of one church, in Pasadena, preaching, proclaiming and transmitting the love and power and challenge of God to people. This one thing he would do, above all else. He labored over his sermons as few of us labor, yet never did he neglect his people, his responsibilities as pastor and administrator. He needed and was given a fine staff which took care of many of the essential tasks which such a church demanded, but while he delegated details to this staff he kept the reins in his hands. It was not his sermon labor alone that wore him out too soon; it was that plus his involvement with, and concern for, his people and for the intense and pressing problems—personal, moral and social—of his church, his community and his country. He worked to create understanding between both sides in a schoolteachers' strike and in a garbagemen's strike. He was both good preacher and good pastor—a combination not often found in any one minister.

His church appreciated this, and much as his people loved to hear him preach, they set him free, four months out of every twelve, to preach in other pulpits all across the country. Wise and supremely Christian, they wanted to share him with the rest of the nation.

He picked up his lamp and took to the road. He preached in nearly every state in the Union, at half a hundred Methodist annual conferences, to conventions and conferences and assemblies in who knows how many other denominations, on a circuit of summer assembly grounds (Masanetta, Junaluska, Ocean City, Ocean Grove, Silver Bay), in colleges and famous churches and in little churches on side roads off Main Street. The call to come and preach was to him like an umpire shouting, "Play ball!" But he was always glad to come back to his

15

Pasadena people, and Pasadena was glad. One of his congregation said, "Whenever Dr. Hamilton comes back, it's like Christmas morning."

Fame and popularity built like snowdrifts around him, but he seemed blissfully unaware of that. Bishop Henley said, "I never knew a man so meek." One night at a banquet, someone remarked that Mrs. Hamilton didn't act like a great preacher's wife; she replied, "How can I? He doesn't know he's a great preacher." Never will his publishers forget the time they had with him when they asked him to autograph his first book in a department store book shop. That is par for the course, with most writers, and most of them like it. But Ham wanted no part of it: "Me? You want me to sit there like a king on a throne? No. I can't do it. I'm not that good. I'm no Hemingway." It took a month to get him to do it, and he wasn't happy when he did it.

Other preachers borrowed his sermons, or parts of them, often word for word. One brother helped himself liberally and even published it over his own name, with no credit whatever; a blistering letter was prepared by the publishers, reminding the offender that he was not only guilty of conduct unbecoming a minister but that he had broken the copyright law as well. Something told us that we had better check with Ham before mailing it, and so we checked, and so the letter was never mailed. Over the phone he said, "No. I don't want that. It would do no good. In a way, I'm glad that the ideas I am trying to express are getting around and being used." When Bishop Pendergrass talked with him about the plagiarizing preachers, he laughed and said, "Well, why shouldn't they? If

16

those sermons are worth all the time I put on them, why shouldn't others benefit by them?"

This was humility. And greatness.

We were stirred to a subtle excitement by the magic of his words; we stood in admiration if not in awe of this probing, brilliant mind and of the burning of his spirit. But in our moments of quiet remembering we see him sitting in that study, *listening*. We call him an idea preacher, a topical or situation preacher, but we would be nearer the truth were we to call him a listening preacher. He listened for the guidance of a Voice that made his own voice poetic, musical, relevant—an echo of the Voice divine. He listened to the heartbeat of mankind, to its problems, hatreds, loves, aspirations, longings and goals; he listened to the lost ones, the doubtful and afraid ones, to scholars and shopkeepers, philosophers, theologians, historians, to the old and the young. Merrily E. Taylor, a member of his church, has written of him, "When you, an awkward and unattractive fifteen or so, went up to speak to him after the service, he listened to you as gravely as if you had been chairman of the board." He listened to people—to the hearts of people—and from those hearts came his preaching.

His friend Halford Luccock wrote him, "You are using up too much strength. You are under 'A Great Compulsion' to save it—to put less of a strain on your physical and nervous capital. . . . You must rein in the wild horses you are riding and make them go slower. There is only one of you, you know, and the Lord went to a lot of trouble to make just one of you. There is no pattern left. So watch what you do with the only model."

Slow down? Such men never slow down. They have no brakes. He kept up the pace long after everyone but himself read the signs of strain in his eyes and face, but . . .! In his last days he was in a new enthusiasm over a new series of sermons he wanted to preach on the *Lord's Prayer*; he had discovered some new shades of beauty, some new mountain peaks, in the *Prayer* to which he would direct our eyes. The last sermon of the series was to bear the title, "Forever."

But he preached his last sermon at a pastors' school in Florida, before he could get down to work on the *Prayer*. Much, much more he longed to preach, but at that moment the weary body and the gallant heart could take no more, and he was suddenly gone from us, out and on through the ultimate golden door.

Death, be not proud! You cannot have this man, you cannot silence him. From his heart he set burning fires in innumerable other hearts and lives, and what he said of God and for God still rings in our ears like the sound of a trumpet, and it is no uncertain sound. He left us with new songs to sing. He touched us with a glory as he passed our way—a glory that, like him, somehow cannot die.

FRANK S. MEAD

Contents

The Golden Door: An Appreciation   7

1. The Core of Christianity   21
2. The Motive Power of Hope   34
3. The Hiddenness of God   46
4. Outside the Temple   58
5. Blunders, Bombers and Builders   72
6. Keep Moving   84
7. On a Clear Day You Can See Forever   96
8. The Lure of the Infinite   107
9. What the World is Waiting For   118
10. The Seeking God   128
11. That Muddy Old River   140
12. Finding the Word   152
13. New Patches or New Creations   166
14. All the World's a Stage.   179

1

The Core of Christianity

LUKE *4:16–21*

IN PAUL'S LETTER to Timothy, the Apostle talks about people who have a form of religion but deny the power; or, as translated by Moffatt, "they keep up a form of religion, [but] they will have nothing to do with it as a force" (II Timothy 3:5).

You have heard of Saint Simeon Stylites. He lived in Antioch in the fifth century. He was a holy man, a Christian who wanted to do the will of God, so for ten years he lived in a narrow cell to get away from the wicked world. But he could not get away from the world there, and he came out of his cell and built for himself a stone pillar, so he could get *above* the world. Up and up he built his pillar, until at sixty feet he felt he was high enough above the world to be safe from its contamination. There he fasted, prayed and lived for more than thirty years. The historian W. E. H. Lecky said he was the ideal Christian of his time, the model Christian of his day.

It is said that on the eve of the Bolshevik revolution, those ten days that shook the world, a congress of Russian priests met in Moscow for a two-day conference on the liturgy of the Church. Six blocks from the place where the first shots of the revolution were fired, these priests were

21

in debate—the issue being whether a white or yellow surplice should be worn in a certain part of the service!

One of the most discouraging facts that church history reveals is the irrelevance of so much that is called Christian, the failure of vast numbers of Christ's followers to understand what Christianity is or what Jesus came to do or what the whole thing is about.

The minister of a downtown church lay dying, and from his bed he wrote this message to his congregation: "Never move your church from its present location. The church makes a great mistake when it gets on a side street." But from the days of Jesus until now this has been the church's consistent blunder, to get on side streets, to get away from the center, to place major emphasis on marginal matters, and to repeat the errors of the Pharisees with whom Jesus continually clashed because they were always on the side street, keeping up the little forms of religion, neglecting the weightier matters and the inner force of what the whole thing was about.

You have heard about the War of the Lilliputians, those little people of Jonathan Swift's satire. Thousands of those little people were killed in a war, the issue of which was whether a boiled egg should be opened at the big end or the little end. I cannot remember now whether the little-enders won over the big-enders, but I do recall that, as I read the story all my sympathy was with the little-enders because that is the party I have always belonged to. How many little matters has the church made central!

When I was a boy, there was a church in my home town in which the people were very holy. They preached holiness, and their holiness consisted largely in the fact that they wore no jewelry, no neckties, no outer adornment—that was what the Almighty was concerned about. Side streets! Recently the Episcopalians had a convention in which they discussed union with the Presbyterians; and they got so bogged down with secondary issues that one of their number reporting the proceedings said, "Any connection between this conference and Christianity is purely coincidental." Side streets!

We cannot live on side streets any more. We have to find the center again. In our lifetime we see a retreat from organized religion. One nation formerly Christian has officially repudiated Christianity, at least in part, because religion was on the side street. Everywhere there is a sifting process going on in the church. We have to determine now how much of this ecclesiastical business is Christian and how much of it is just accumulation; or, to use Paul's phrase, we have to determine what the forms of faith are and what really constitutes the force of it. Christianity is not a form. It uses forms and has to have them, but it has come down across the generations as a living, vital, moving force. What is that force?

Thomas Carlyle in 1840 wrote of the preacher of his day expressing the wish that he could find the point again, this preaching man, and stick to it, for there is need of him yet—this speaking function, this truth coming to us in a living voice has a perennial place—if he could but find the point again. What is the point of it? What is the core of Christianity? What is the inner force of this faith of ours as distinguished from its external forms?

I would like to divide our thought into two sections

which are really not two things but two parts of the same thing. Put down first the *forgiveness of sin*. I am sure of that. I believe the first and most potent force of the Christian movement as it has been released through twenty centuries is in the area of moral transformation— the cure of sin, the transformation of the inner life. All the world's religions begin with the inner wrongness in the human heart and seek to find some saving cure for it. Nothing is right until it is right at the heart. Our word *gospel* means good news, and this is the good news—now we have redemption through His blood, even the forgiveness of our sins. That is the word that rings like music through the New Testament. That was the impulse in which the Christian church was born. That was what the apostles preached with a kind of delirious joy. That was the force that propelled it across the Roman Empire, bringing hope to people who lived in the grip of fatalism, and bringing what Lecky called "a new morality" into European life. That was what commended the Gospel to our own rough ancestors in the Tin Islands, and gradually changed the character of the Anglo-Saxon world. The love of God is forgiveness and the transformation of the inner life.

John Bunyan put it in a little picture in a book, which came in England to be second only to the Bible, *Pilgrim's Progress*. If you have forgotten the picture, let me paraphrase it for you: In my dream I saw a man clothed with rags, with a book in his hand and a great burden on his back. I saw him run up the highway, not without great difficulty because of the burden on his back. But when he came to the Cross, the burden loosed from his shoulders, fell from his back into the sepulcher, and I saw it no more. Then he gave three leaps for joy and went on singing. In that little picture John Bunyan was really writing the history of the English-speaking world. England was the man clothed in rags with a great burden on his back. The whole Anglo-Saxon race was lifted up from savagery by the light and power of the cross. You can trace it in our hymns. Look through the hymn books that our forefathers made and see how often somebody is bursting into song because of One who breaks the power of cancelled sin and sets the prisoner free.

> At the cross, at the cross, where I first
>   saw the light
> And the burden of my heart rolled away.
> It was there by faith that I first saw the light
> And now I am happy all the day.

The forgiveness of sin!

Now if this old Bunyan picture seems queer to us and if the word *sin*, as the late Archbishop Temple said, has for our generation vague meaning and scant understanding, it is not because the reality of sin has lessened: it is mostly because we are calling sin by other names and seeking to cure it by other means. Our religious vocabulary has been rewritten by psychologists, and we have changed the pattern of our thinking. Substitute maladjustment for the word sin and the burden is still on our backs. Substitute frustration for what our fathers called conviction, substitute neurosis for what the Bible called a demon, and modern man is still a pilgrim with a great burden on his back, only he is not looking to a cross to lift it. He turns to amusement to forget it, or to bromides to deaden it, or he goes to the psychiatrist, if he can afford it, to get his twist straightened out. We have a whole new priesthood, and a new vocabulary for the reality of sin. A tranquilizer is what you take for heartbreak.

No, we haven't got rid of sin by redefining it. We are still a burdened people, great multitudes of mixed-up men and women struggling up the road with a great burden on our backs. What a wonderful release would come to our hearts and homes if we could find the point again, find once more the core of it. When his burden fell off, Bunyan's pilgrim "gave three leaps for joy and went on singing." What a lift would come to the world's life, what a cleansing of its moral soul, if we could recover the inner force of it, even though we might have to change some of the forms in which it is expressed. I am convinced we have to do that. In every age we have had to get back of the forms and the words to recover the reality of what we started out to say. You can see it in the Gospels. You can see it in the story of Zacchaeus, the little man who climbed into the sycamore tree. When Jesus saved Zacchaeus there was a lift through the whole community—*everybody* felt it. This little man found forgiveness, and it changed him. He was crooked and he became straight. He was stingy and he became generous. "Behold, Lord, the half of my goods," he said, "I give to the poor; and if I have taken any thing from any man by false accusation, I restore him fourfold" (Luke 19:8). See it? Fifty percent of his

26

income to missions and restitution at the rate of four hundred percent! There is something quite practical about forgiveness.

In Wisconsin I once helped to get an old man converted, and he was so glad, so grateful, that he wanted to give me his horse. It was all I could do to keep him from giving me that horse. What would I do with a horse? That was a long time ago: I might take it now. Religion makes people big. It makes them joyous and generous and open-handed and openhearted. There is something very practical and very *exciting* about forgiveness.

There is a story about Zacchaeus after his conversion in the sycamore tree. He behaved so strangely that his wife was alarmed by what she thought were symptoms of insanity. Every morning instead of going down to his business, as a sane man ought to do, he set off in the opposite direction with a spade in his hand and a water jar under his arm. Finally, she became so curious she followed him. (The most curious thing in this world is a woman who isn't.) She saw him go down to the village well and fill the jar with water, then out through the village path to that old sycamore tree. Scraping away the rubbish and the dirt, he poured the water over its roots and stood there stroking its trunk with his hand. Out of her hiding place came his wife for an explanation. "I found Him here," he said. "Here is where I found Him."

Is there a tree in your life somewhere, some spot sacred because you found Him there? If you have not found this, if you have not come to grips with this, then you have not found the core of it yet. You may have a form of religion,

27

but you have not experienced the inner force of it, for this is what the religion of Christ is first of all about—the cure of sin, and the transformation of the inner life.

What then? With the sins forgiven and the unclean spirit driven out—what then? Is that it, all of it? Any sincere search for the core of Christianity will lead inevitably to a synagogue in Nazareth where Jesus stated very plainly what He had come to do. "The Spirit of the Lord is upon me, because he hath anointed me"—to *do* something. What? It is precisely at this point where millions of people have missed the point. Many people have said, "The Spirit of the Lord is upon me: I'm saved," and stopped there. They put a period there. Religious experience is unrelated to personal piety, and such people are blissfully detached from the major issues which are the social issues of life. Much of our Christianity is like that—people who stop too soon, getting on side streets, and developing a form of religion in which it is God's chief business to take care of them, to furnish them a happy thought every day and solve their personal problems. That, however vital and important, is only the beginning.

The world today has looked at this form of religion and spurned it, calling it opiate because that is what unrelated religion is—dope, not dynamics. Most of us know now that we have made our Christianity too small a thing, put limits on it, failed to grasp its wider dimension, the universal social force and the progressive nature of faith. Into the vacuum we have poured all sorts of spurious panaceas. "The Spirit of the Lord is upon me," Jesus said. Then He follows a program of social concerns that touches the total life of man: sight for the blind, healing for the hurt, good news for the poverty-stricken, liberty for the oppressed. See it? All the dreams that stirred in Him were linked up with man's great social hopes, and all the power of God in Him was dedicated to their fulfillment in the enlargement of the human spirit.

That is what Christianity is: a living vital force in life to move it from center to circumference. This to Him was the Kingdom of God; and His challenge to "follow me" in that day was a bugle call to earnest men to make it happen on earth. "Thy Kingdom come," He said, "Thy will be done on earth." You see Him pick His disciples, gather these young Galileans around Him, and for three years fill their minds with new ideas, new hopes and new thoughts about God and life. It was like new wine, He said, which would burst the old wineskins and demand new ones to contain it. Jesus believed without doubt that His spirit moving in the minds of men would bring about social changes and it is the miracle of history that it did just that.

There are three great social convictions that run through all the teachings of Jesus. You will not find them listed one, two, three in the Gospels, but they are the core of His message; and around these basic convictions most, if not all, of the teachings of Jesus cluster. The fatherhood of God is the first. Everything He said was rooted in that, in God the loving, sustaining Spirit of all created things. Second is the solidarity of life—the oneness of man. Call it brotherhood, if you like. Humanity is one. A third grows out of the other two: the sacredness of a person— the dignity of the individual. These clustered ideas are not just theological pronouncements. They are social convictions which have been woven into history and, bit by bit, across the centuries wrought in our western institutions. You cannot walk a block on any street without running into some expression of this living force as it has taken form in our civilization.

Take the dignity of man, for example. James Russell Lowell said that there is enough dynamite in that one idea to blast all of our existing systems to atoms, which is precisely what it is doing now. In the great social surge of our time, everywhere men are reaching up for dignity, for respect, for better life. The fact is, it has always done this. See it in the past coming into contact with all those old tyrannies, autocracies and slaveries! You see it emancipate women and throw protection around the children. You see it build institutions of mercy and institutions of the mind. You see it as the impulse in what Edmund Burke called the fierce spirit of liberty.

I once stood in that old frame church in Richmond, Virginia, with its old-fashioned, boxed-in pews. I shut my eyes and heard a man say again, "Give me liberty or give me death"; and I thought how fitting it was that he said it in a church, for that's where it was born—not on a battlefield, not in a political rally, but in the matrix of man's stubborn faith. It did not start in Richmond nor Valley Forge nor Philadelphia. You see its beginning way back in Egypt, where Moses, believing in the living God and that man was made in His likeness, set out to make his people free. "Let my people go." The fierce spirit of liberty has always been at the core of our Hebrew-Christian faith.

The Romans complained that Jews and Christians did

30

not make good slaves because something in their fanatical religion made them unfit to be subjugated. Thank God! People who believe they are created in the likeness of God never make good slaves to anyone. Why does the Ku Klux Klan burn churches in Mississippi? Because out of the churches comes the fierce spirit of liberty. This cluster of ideas moved through the misty maze of European life, germinating in men's minds until they were obliged to coin new words for their political vocabulary and build new forms and structures for their inner vitality. New bottles for a new wine!

These ideals have changed the mental climate of the world. It is largely this cluster of ideas which makes up the texture of democracy—not wholly, for other factors enter in—but just try to imagine democracy without them. Take out of democracy the idea of brotherhood, the idea that the strong have some responsibility for the weaker brother. Take out of democracy the sacredness of the person, the dignity of man, the rights of the individual, and what is left? Not much! Mostly an empty form is left from which the living force is gone. Democracy is an attempt—and I guess the most promising attempt yet made—to give political expression to the social ideals of the Kingdom of God, and you see where it gets us.

Every so often someone complains that America has no ideology, no thought-out national philosophy. The strength of totalitarian states, the argument goes, lies in the fact that they have an ideology, a set of ideas to which they are committed, a thought-out purpose that holds them together and gives them a great driving force. Count Herman Alexander Keyserling said that we are too young, that America is still a colony, a people not yet a nation, a body but not yet a soul. We have no thought-out national purpose, no ideology. Haven't we? This is the forgotten ideology of America, these clusters of ideas, these basic convictions. This was the inner force around which America was organized. This was the impulse out of which the whole New World came into being. America, said Calvin Coolidge, was born out of a religious revival. He meant the Renaissance, the Reformation and all those rumblings in the Old World that brought the pilgrims across the roaring sea. Every nation is built around something, around certain basic ideas which form the heartbeat of the nation. Certainly in the making of what Jefferson called the American mind, and what Adams called the American dream, these were the inner forces, however imperfectly they were held and however inadequately they were grasped. All men before God equal and endowed by their creator—this was the truth they dared to build around, and they felt, like ancient Israel, that they were the pioneers of a new idea and the custodians of it for the rest of mankind.

We could quote at length on this. John Adams said in 1765, "I always consider the settlement of America with wonder and reverence as the opening of a grand scene and design for . . . the . . . emancipation of . . . mankind. No country was ever founded on deeper religious foundations."

It is still in us. We have not lost it. The core of it is still there. We still respond to it when it is called democracy. When the flag goes by we confess it as our faith, and we can be roused to defend it when it is threatened. We have forgotten only the source of it, that is all: we have forgotten the inner force that produced it, and we are perilously neglecting the roots of it. That is what gives point to our concern in our modern church-and-state dilemma—that we should be forced to bring our children up through an educational process that is not permitted to teach the source of it but strips them of all thought of it.

Deep within us is the hope that our excursion into secularism is a temporary lapse, that we shall come to our senses again, think it through and understand more clearly that we cannot have these social fruits without their spiritual roots, that we cannot have the good world that we want without being the good people God wants. We are people with a thousand years of Christian teaching in our minds. We are the descendants of people who looked into the face of Christ, were lifted out of savagery by His light and came to this New World to make His dream come true. We cannot forget that overnight, and we *must not* forget. Our deepest wish is that America will be like the young soldier in the Civil War who got sick on the battlefield and was taken to the hospital tent. Lying there on a cot, he pleaded with the doctor, "Oh, doctor, don't tell me I'm not fit for duty. Don't tell me I can't go back. It's only a touch of the fever, Doc, and the sound of the bugle will make me well again." This is what the whole world is listening for—a lifting up of a great purpose, a clear and positive blast on the bugle of the living God.

2

The Motive Power of Hope

ROMANS *15*

"FOR WHATEVER was written in former days was written for our instruction, that . . . by the encouragement of the scriptures we might have hope" (Romans 15:4, RSV).

Dr. Halford Luccock tells about a company of people having dinner together. One of the party was just back from a vacation in Maine. He told his friends a poignant story of a little village in the hills which was doomed to extinction. The state was building a power dam on the river and had bought up the surrounding property that, with the completion of the dam in a year or so, would be flooded by a large lake. The effect on the little village was quite demoralizing. Everything suddenly came to a standstill. All building stopped, of course, and all improvement and repair stopped. What was the use of painting a house if, in a year or so, it would be covered with water? Why repair anything or replace anything when the whole village was certain to be wiped out? So month by month the town became dilapidated, bedraggled and ghostly, and the man commenting on it said, "Where there is no faith in the future, there is no power in the present."

That story is a rather penetrating little parable of the plight and predicament of millions in our world today.

Where there is no faith in the future, there is no power in the present.

One day I made a discovery. I realized I had never preached a sermon on the word *hope*. I suppose it was because I assumed hope, or took it for granted. We need to be exhorted frequently to have faith, and be reminded often to build love into life. But hope—hope is a natural virtue, as instinctive as a cry, it "springs eternal in the human breast," wrote Alexander Pope. Who needs to be preached to about hope? Not American people, certainly. We are hopeful people, just naturally hopeful; it is in our blood. Everyone among us, Christian or unchristian, takes it for granted that hope is a good thing, a virtue without which life would be dreadful and not worth living.

Then I made another discovery, as I studied the place of hope in history. Not always has hope been regarded as a virtue. We don't realize at all how much our hopeful way of thinking about life, which we think is natural in us, is rooted in Bible religion and is the result of centuries of Christian teaching. We are hopeful because we have been brought up in a land with an atmosphere that is hopeful. We get quite a shock to discover that in most pagan cultures it is not so. Hope is not thought of as a virtue to be desired, but an evil to be shunned. In the philosophies of India today—in Buddhism, for example—hope is not considered a virtue. It is regarded as a deceiver, a betrayer and a will-o'-the-wisp that leads men astray; and the secret of wisdom is to get rid of hope, or, if you indulge in it at all, it is to hope for nirvana (extinction), which is a long way from what we Christians mean by hope.

The same is true of that old Mediterranean world into

which Christianity came. It was a world, as Paul said, "having no hope and without God" (Ephesians 2:12, RSV); that is, Greeks and Romans did not fool themselves with hope. They did not trust it. They never put it in their list of virtues. Do you remember the old story of Pandora? When she opened her beautiful box and released all the evils on the world, she left one evil in the bottom, and that evil was hope. Of course they had their short-range hopes, as all people do, but hope for the future was not in their thinking. What was the use to hope for the future when history, as Plato taught, was just going around and around in cycles—going nowhere? How surprised that old fatalistic world must have been to hear of this new religion that spoke of hope as an unqualified virtue, linking it with faith and love as one of the three principal graces.

The Bible from beginning to end regards hope as an unquestionable good. The history of Israel is the history of a great hope. The prophets believed in the future and in the coming of a great day—a kingdom of good, the Kingdom of God when "the earth will be filled with the knowledge of the glory of the Lord, as the waters cover the sea" (Habakkuk 2:14, RSV). In the New Testament that note of hope is vastly heightened. "Blessed be the God and Father of our Lord Jesus Christ [who] . . . hath begotten us again unto a [living] hope by the resurrection of Jesus Christ" (I Peter 1:3). Paul tells us we are the people with a hope. We rejoice in a hope. "Ye sorrow not even as others which have no hope" (I Thessalonians 4:13). To him God was the source of it. He was the God of hope, and everything that was written in the Scriptures, he said, "was written for our instruction, that . . . by the

36

encouragement of the scriptures we might have hope" (Romans 15:4, RSV).

Certainly there is no doubt about this. The Gospel of Christ came as the good news of hope. It had a hopeful view of God, a hopeful view of man and a hopeful view of history. History is not just going around and around. It is moving toward a goal. The goal is the Kingdom of our God and His Christ.

And there is no doubt about this either: this hopeful view of life has exercised a powerful influence on the whole thought of the western world for two thousand years, saturating our minds and energizing our hands, until hope among us is taken for granted as a virtue.

What has gone wrong with it? What has happened to hope? Hope has taken a terrible beating in the last half century. We have seen so many hopes fail, and so many high expectations go out one by one like candles sputtering in the wind, until hope has become a rare commodity. When we listen to the thinkers talk now about the future, we hear echoes of that pagan thought, that pre-Christian fatalism, and that old Greek notion of impending tragedy and recurring doom that make our hopes a mockery.

What has happened to hope? What has happened to change the mood of optimism, with which the century began, to one of pessimism, fear and near despair? If we could get the answer to that, we could get our feet on solid ground again and at least part of the answer is clear enough. For one thing, we have become shallow in our hopes. More and more we have been turning away from the deep spiritual meanings of great words and squeezing the moral content out of them until in that process, hope, like freedom, has become a shallow, secular, superficial thing—little more than an amiable disposition to look on the bright side.

In *South Pacific*, Mary Martin sang, "I'm stuck like a dope, with a thing called hope." While that is lovely sentiment, it is not exactly what the New Testament means by hope. The expressions *all will be well, hope for the best*, and *look on the bright side* are mostly sentiment. It is like a little boy who stood with his father at the window of a pet shop to pick out a puppy for his birthday present. They stood there looking at the little doggies in the window. Finally the father asked, "Have you picked one yet, son?"

"Yes, Dad, I have," pointing to one little puppy furiously wagging his tail. "I want the one with the happy ending."

Well, who doesn't? We all believe in happy endings. There is no particular virtue in it, but that is what hope has come to mean for many—hope divorced from its moral meaning, substitutes cheerfulness, optimism and belief in happy endings.

We have been putting our faith in a lot of false hopes—secular hopes that have no root in reality. We have believed a lot of things that are not so and we have deceived ourselves with false hopes. We have believed in something we call progress. We are not sure what it means but it is a nice word, pleasant to think about—that everything is getting better and better and that we are in a cosmic movement upward from a lower level to a higher level. If human progress is automatically assured, if it is set in the mechanism of life itself and if the transition from savagery to civilization is predestined and mechanically determined, certainly we do not need God in that process. Why fool with the Bible or worry about our sins or bother trying to love our neighbor if we can be good by automation? All we need to do is to turn our faces to the East three times a day and repeat the ritual: "Now are we the sons of Darwin and it doth not yet appear what we shall be."

Something has happened to that hope. This world is too tough and too evil to yield to our mechanical over-simplifications. Whatever else progress is, it is not mechanical and it is not automatic. The events of life have shattered that illusion.

A similar fate is now overtaking some other forms of secular optimism to which men have turned as substitutes for the Christian hope. Scientific humanism, for instance —how optimistically have we believed in it! What almost blind trust we have put in science to be the saviour, to solve our problems and to usher in the rosy world of the millennium. It is a false hope. Science is a wonderful tool, destined to be still more wonderful, but as a saviour, it has some definite limitations. In fact it is the very triumph of science—science divorced from Christian meanings and human values—that fills us with fear now about the future.

Or take Communism—what a vast hoax that is. It is a worldwide deception covering nearly half the earth. How many millions have been bewitched and then betrayed by the hope it held out! The ideas of Marx and Lenin loomed up at first for millions of depressed people as a bright light in their darkness. It looked so good: it promised so much. It was the secular world's substitute for the Kingdom of God. It provided them with a hope which at first seemed not ill-founded: by throwing off old superstitions, man by himself—man without God, by his own planning and human effort—could create Utopia here and bring about a perfect world society. Something has happened to that hope. How much disillusionment has come out of it and how much is yet to come out of it!

We could go on and on. There are many forms of secular optimism. One false hope after another and one light after another shines up and goes out, until we have a world now that is afraid to hope. All through Europe we have the nihilistic movement—people whose religion is to believe in nothing. They have seen so many hopes go down that they have made peace with hopelessness and believe in nothing. In America the Beat generation—mixed-up kids—stood on street corners talking about the end of the world. The clear, logical situation did not seem to dawn on them, that if they put their faith in illusions, they could expect to be disillusioned. If our hopes have let us down, it is because they have been falsely placed. That does not seem to register. We are getting a world now like that pre-Christian world which Paul said was without God and therefore without hope.

An unfortunate part of the situation is that these deceptive expectations were shared by many Christian people. The Christian church in many areas became identified with these secular hopes until some have come to think that the Christian hope itself is a delusion.

What to do about that? Where is the rock for our feet? Where is the road to confidence again? Here it is, at least in part. For one thing, we must clarify the Christian hope and disassociate it from the secular substitutes and empty optimisms that pervert it. We must root it deeply again in the realm where hopes hold steady. We Christians have no business putting faith in the world's illusions, or losing our hopefulness when these man-made dreams turn out to be deceptive. We ought to know where our real hope lies. "Why art thou cast down, O my soul? and why art thou disquieted in me? hope thou in God" (Psalm 42:5) —that is it! Our hopefulness is based not in the dreams and schemes of men, but in the nature and character of God. "My hope is built on nothing less," as the hymn says. If a Christian loses his hopefulness, it is simply because he has misplaced his hope and tried to build it on something less.

There is a well-known story of Martin Luther. This man who had the courage to stand unflinchingly before popes and kings once fell into a spell of despondency that he could not shake for days. One morning his wife came down to breakfast dressed in deep mourning. She wore a black dress. She closed the windows, locked the door and tiptoed in silence around the house. Luther watched her with bewilderment for awhile and then he asked: "Is somebody dead?" She said, "Yes. Don't you know, Martin? God! God is dead!" The old rugged German took the hint and snapped out of it. He had sense enough to know that anyone whose hope is centered in an eternal God cannot go moping around in mourning. The motive power of hope!

"No army," said a British statesman, "can march on a retreating mind." That is to say, you cannot live without hope. No society—no civilization—can endure creatively without hope. Where there is no faith in the future, there is no power in the present. If men ever become convinced —*really* convinced—that there is nothing worthwhile in what they do and that it will all come to nothing at the last, they will soon stop doing it. Like that village in Maine, the earth will become a ghostly place. If research doctors, for example, ever become convinced, or even suspicious, that there could be no cure for cancer—no answer, no solution to the puzzle—their quest would flag and the power would go out of their hands. "We are saved," Paul said, "by hope" (Romans 8:24). And it is the business of Christian people to lift up in this tired world the light of hope—hope that is centered in God, hope that there is a solution. However obscure the puzzle, however hard the fight, there is an answer, because at the center of it there is God who has shown us His will and way in Christ the Lord.

It's all in the hymn we sing.

> On Christ, the solid Rock, I stand;
> All other ground is sinking sand.
>
> EDWARD MOTE

All other ground! That is what we must do: we must clarify the Christian hope, making clear the difference between what is rock and what is sand.

We must see it in its right perspective. The Christian hope is certainly not for people who have a jackpot complex, or for people who want everything to happen immediately, if not sooner. We are not encouraged to trust in panaceas or quick-change magic. We simply cannot change social patterns or human hearts with the same speed with which we can turn out new models in automobiles or even spaceships to the moon. Perhaps it is no wonder at all that our moral wisdom lags so far behind our mechanical progress.

People who are saturated with the Bible concept of hope have learned from it the gift of patience, the long look, the abiding trust that can work and wait. One summer at the Silver Bay Association on Lake George, New York, I had a brief talk with Dr. Martin Niemöller, who seemed to be a symbol of Christian triumph, Christian patience and Christian confidence in a world of turmoil. He spent most of the war years in a concentration camp as Hitler's personal prisoner. He was a kind of Daniel in a Nazi Babylon, with his windows opened toward the city of God. To see him, to hear him talk, you could hardly believe that this quiet little man could have done it—that he could have challenged and defied the Nazi monsters. He watched Germany plunge down the path to national ruin. He watched his native land move away from the strong principles that had shaped it and follow a mad policy of Christ-denial and rejection. Yet when he talked about Hitler and his goons, he did not get red in the face, nor shout, nor even raise his voice. He had this quality of quiet courage born of an abiding confidence in the eternity of God. He seemed to be listening to the tick of an astronomical clock, knowing that the centuries were God's, whatever the years seemed to say. When Hitler stood before him shouting, threatening and foam-

43

ing at the mouth, he calmly said, "Because there is God, *Mein Fuehrer*, we can wait. But we cannot give to man the things which are God's to save our bodies and lose our souls."

That is the authentic voice of the Christian hope. "Because there is God, we can wait!" The Kingdom of God is not a divine gift that drops down suddenly from the skies, nor is it a simple human task to be completed in a generation or two. It is the eternal call of God to every man in his brief moment of time to stand up and stand out, and something happens to our hope when we learn to listen to what the centuries are saying against the years.

Something happens to it, too, when we put our hands to a task. Dr. Albert Schweitzer once said that when he got to brooding over things and was inclined to be pessimistic about the way things were going, and when he began to lose his hope, he always got up to do something, to get his hands on something and to do something ever so little to lessen the evil in God's world. That did something helpful to his spirit. Perhaps it is no accident that those who are voicing the deepest pessimism today are the philosophers, the thinkers, the poets, the novelists and some theologians—people who are sitting in cloistered studies brooding, or discussing problems academically where they are remote from life. I have never known a missionary who was pessimistic for very long. The people who are grappling with the hard tasks seem to be incurably hopeful. That ought to mean something. We would be a more hopeful, happy and joyful people if we would do less sitting around. Pitch in somewhere: get your hands on something. The hands have a lot to do with hope.

One night our family saw a play on television; it was the dramatization of a true story, a kidnapping which took place in San Francisco. A young businessman from a well-to-do family was kidnapped by a couple of professional hoodlums and held for ransom in a hideaway in the city. The suspense in the drama was created by the part the newspapers played. The district attorney called the newsmen together, asked their cooperation. He also asked them to do an unusual thing—not to print anything until the police could have a chance to find the victim and his abductors. The newspapermen agreed to keep an absolute blackout on all news of the kidnapping, as though they did not know anything about it. One leak—the slightest hint in the newspapers that the police knew of the plot— would have meant death for the young man. It was fascinating to watch those newsmen restrain the impulse to print the news in order to save a man's life. We could see the spirit of the thing take hold of them until they were more excited about saving that man's life than getting news out of it. When the search was successfully ended, a hard-bitten city editor sat at his desk, saying, "For twenty-five years I've been writing stories about life. This is the first time I've had a part in making the story come out right."

There's excitement in that—having some part in making the story come out right. Something happens to our hopefulness when we come in off the sidelines to take up the task and have some share in making God's story come true.

3

The Hiddenness of God

EXODUS *33:18–23;* JOHN *14:5–10*

ONE OF THE DEEP and trustworthy insights of Biblical religion, in the Old Testament and the New, is linked up with the silence, the hiddenness of God.

"Oh, that I knew where I might find Him" (23:3, RSV), Job cried out in his torment.

"Behold, I go forward, but he is not there; and backward, but I cannot perceive him; on the left hand I seek him, but I cannot behold him; I turn to the right hand, but I cannot see him" (23:8 RSV). "Verily," said Isaiah, "thou art a God that hidest thyself" (45:15).

"Why standest thou afar off" (Psalm 10:1).

In the New Testament, Philip voices the same wistful question of Jesus. "Show us the Father," he said, "and we shall be satisfied" (John 14:8 RSV).

These and many other passages in the Scriptures speak of moments in human experience when God seems distant, absent or even nonexistent. The records are full of it, and somehow we've got to deal with that, because it's an experience which is our own. In fact today it's what constitutes one of the major arguments of unbelief—the absence, the unknown whereabouts of God. It has become a sophisticated subject for far-out theology and it has provided the theme of any number of secular plays, principal among them Samuel Beckett's ambiguous fantasy *Waiting for Godot*, an odd story about two nondescript hobos waiting around for someone who never shows up. (It played sixteen months to packed theaters in the capitals of Europe.) A vague mysterious person has promised to meet them there and never comes, or if he came in disguise they didn't recognize him. Even the writer accused of some of the dirtiest books on the newsstand, Henry Miller, in an interview for a religious magazine, said that we are now passing through a period of cosmic insensitivity, a period when God seems more and more absent and man is doomed to come face to face with the fate he has created for himself.

The absent God—the God who doesn't appear or who comes in ways we do not recognize! Why should we be surprised at all by this talk of absence? We could have learned it from the Bible. Centuries ago Isaiah said, "Verily, thou art a God that hidest thyself." Let's head into that.

Let's remember, first, that this is the God we perceive in nature, the God who never appears. Who has ever seen Him? We may wish for some assurance here, but the Almighty doesn't give it. He doesn't advertise Himself or put a sign on every rose bush reading THIS COMES THROUGH THE COURTESY OF THE ALMIGHTY. He doesn't put His label on every summer shower like the advertisers of soap and detergent, WHITER THAN WHITE. He is always the Invisible behind the visible, the unseen Mover behind the motion. We are confronted in nature with a certain automatic element, with all things moving without an apparent Mover. The world seems to operate under its own steam. The seasons come and go without our help; the earth turns around every day; the heat of the sun lifts water from the sea, and when the clouds are chilled, the rain falls; the grass grows green to manufacture food to keep all living things alive. It is all so simple, self-regulating and automatic that much of our modern thinking about nature, because of its consistent regularity, has seemed to move in the direction of eliminating the very idea of the necessity of God. Who needs Him? The thing runs itself. *This* causes *that*, and that's it. The Mover never shows up.

We are confronted, too, with an element of purpose. Every living organism and every individual cell has a bit of intelligence in it, something akin to our own minds, and seems to know within itself what it's supposed to do or be. Something pushes a palm seed to become a palm tree. It never makes a mistake to become a pumpkin, and from the moment it touches the soil it seems to know within itself what its needs are and how to meet them. It lifts a hundred tons of sap every season into its branches to make its blossoms and its cluster of seeds keeps palm trees coming on. By its own built-in intelligence it moves to its own creative end. Where is the Mind behind the mind, the Power that does the pushing? We never see it. The Pusher never shows up.

There's an amazing chemistry in everything, but we never see the Chemist. There's a mathematical order in the movement of the stars so accurate we set our clocks by it, but the Engineer never comes out to take a bow. There's beauty in the order.

The artistry is here. Where is the Artist? The scientist today sees the universe as a single living process, a web of life in which all things are linked together with a maze of laws so intricate and interwoven, so far-reaching and complex, that no human mind can hold it in totality. It's not only bigger than we imagine, it's bigger than we *can* imagine; and yet the Organizer, the Architect of the great design, never makes a speech to tell us how it's done. Even its laws are so deftly hidden it takes almost genius to discover them. He is hidden even in His presence.

A man from Florida brought a lawsuit against "God and Company" when an insurance firm denied his claim for damages in an accident on the grounds that it was an act of God. So he brought suit against God and Company and named as co-defendants the churches of the city who claimed to be God's representatives. The court dismissed the case as disrespectful. The Defendant didn't show up, but that's intriguing. If you had a case against the Almighty, whom would you sue? Where would you find Him? Where in all this vast creation can we see the face of its Creator? Nowhere!

The Soviets sent a spaceship spinning around the earth and came back saying He wasn't out there. They looked for Him, but saw no paradise, no angels, no Heavenly Father—nothing but space and emptiness. You wonder how they missed Him in the glory of the skies and the grandeur of His creations. You wonder if they expected Him to catch their little balloon and throw it back, or hold it in His hand. There's a story going the rounds among Christian people in Russia that one day the Kremlin sent up a satellite and it didn't come back, and they were worried about that. Then a few days later two of them hung around the pearly gates and asked St. Peter, "Sir, we don't want to come in, but please can we have our ball back?" When we turn to the great immensities we have to say with Isaiah, "Verily, thou art a God that hidest thyself."

There's as much below zero as above it. When we look down to the astronomy of the invisible and to the sub-atomic galaxies of energy, the mystery deepens until men are stricken dumb. We see the glory in a blade of grass, the chemistry of the eyeball, the fluttering throat of a mockingbird, the beating of a rabbit's tiny heart, and down beneath all this is the invisible DNA code that holds in its memory enough information to fill an encyclopedia. It is said by the molecular biologists, the men who know about these things, that the cell may contain half a million molecules. To grasp the chemical organization of the least of them is still far beyond our capacity. Down, in a world we cannot see someone employs chemistry and mathematics that would paralyze a computer. Everywhere we're made conscious of mind, of intelligence unseen and out of sight, of the unknown deeper than the known, and when we search for the Mind behind the mind we hear nothing but the silence and see nothing but the absence. "Verily, thou art a God that hidest thyself."

Sometime ago the world was gently jolted by the news from Capetown, South Africa, that a team of doctors had put a heart of one man into the body of another, and the world marveled at the miracle, as well it should. But what about the first heartbeat? Who performed that one, producing the delicate balance of a chemical pump that goes on working night and day automatically for eighty or ninety years? When some of us went to school a thousand years ago, the professor told us that the atom was the smallest thing imaginable, called so by the Greeks because it was uncuttable. Since then it has been cut and cut again and split again. I heard Dr. William Pollard, at Oak Ridge, trace the exciting journey from the small to the smaller to the smallest. "Just a few years ago," he said, "we adjusted ourselves to a simple satisfying view in which everything . . . was made up of just three elementary constituents, electrons, neutrons, protons. [But] this did not last for long. Soon additional . . . particles were being discovered . . . a whole array of [them], and each particle [had] an anti-particle so that we deal now with matter and anti-matter. [And the possibility is that] at the inner-most chamber of the maze one would find *nothing." No thing*!

It's interesting to note that in 1967 the men who were awarded the Nobel prize in medicine were three doctors who had measured the nearest thing to nothing in the nerve cells—an electronic impulse in the brain that lasts one one-thousandth of a second and carries signals to the body cells. So we don't know any more whether something is matter or energy, or who presides over the organization. How far away is God? Out there where our minds can't stretch, in here where our eyes can't see! Verily, in the world of nature, Thou art a God that hidest Thyself.

Now we must go beyond nature, because it is in the area of human nature and human experience that this hiddenness of God is being tragically confused with non-existence. "The new fact of our time," says William

51

Hamilton, "is the disappearance of God from the human scene. He has withdrawn Himself. He has withdrawn from the world and He is absent from its vital life." In our time that old Nietzschean cry, "God is dead, and we have killed Him," has been pulled out of mothballs to become a byword in our speech.

A little girl in Canada said tearfully to her mother, "I love God, but He's dead." Some say it joyfully, as though they had found release. Some say it sadly, as though they had lost a friend. Some feel it deeply, and have no word to express it. Tennessee Williams in *Sweet Bird of Youth* makes one of his characters say, "I believe that the silence of God, the absolute speechlessness of Him is a long, long and awful thing that the whole world is lost because of." Theology is full of this. Martin Buber wrote a book about *The Eclipse of God*, and even Sartre wrote a play which expresses the frightening absence of God.

I don't know why these sad and lonely thinkers should be so wrought up about the absence of God. We're not wholly in the dark about the why of it, about why God must dwell in mystery, inaccessible. Why should we assume that God should be wholly intelligible to us, that with our little box of brains we can comprehend the infinite or know all about God when we don't know all about anything? We should at least maintain a sense of humor and expect some bewilderment in us and some magnitude in Him beyond the limits of our reach. What sort of God would He be that you and I could get our minds around, or that a college professor could hold in his little skull? Can we measure the sky with a yardstick, shake hands with the Maker of the Milky Way, or, as Job asked, can we catch a whale with a fish hook? A sense of humor would help. It's almost amusing to imagine that we who are creatures of a day, with minds that can't see a day ahead, could measure the majesty of a Mind that created the heavens and the earth and all that in them is. Our minds are simply not made for that dimension. We know in part, we see through a glass darkly, and, as Sir Wilfred Grenfell said, "He who wants all heaven in his head is going to get his head split." Wherever we touch God we touch mystery, and between the finite and the infinite there must always be a veil, something not yet seen, a curtain that never can be lifted.

More than that, there's mercy in the mystery. God should be hidden from our eyes and our senses should be guarded and protected from too much light. T. S. Eliot said that humans can't bear too much reality. We're learning that again in the space age with experiments going on as to how much man can take and what he can't take. We are learning how frail he is against the elements and how fortunate he is that this is a carefully guarded universe in which he is protected, for one thing, by the veil of atmosphere from radiation and from the fires of the sun, and by a thousand unseen curtains from too much breaking in—for which he is not fitted.

The ancients had an expression, "If you can't face the candle, how can you look at the sun?" You wonder sometimes how these men who complain about God's absence could ever stand the fullness of His presence. Just what would they want Him to do, leap into our midst with overwhelming power to solve our problems? Step out on the stars some night and write His name in flaming letters across the sky, "I am the Lord your God. Beside me there is no other"? Suppose He did. We'd blow a fuse! The Old Testament prophet cried, "O that thou wouldst rend the heavens and come down (Isaiah 64:1, RSV). Suppose He did. You have to ask how much of that kind of revelation we could stand. If He should reveal Himself in the fullness of His power, we would shrivel up. We've had a little smidgen of it, a mushroom light against the sky. Men have opened up a small crack in the universe and found a hidden power there, a small hint of other powers that would utterly destroy us if we were not guarded from their light. The veil between the seen and the unseen, between the world that we can stand and live in and the world we could not bear, is very thin, but it is there and there's mercy as well as majesty in the mystery of His hiddenness.

More than that—what a useless, helpless creature man would be with God breaking in to solve his problems! A certain absence of God is essential to man's growth and to the development of his resources. His hiddenness is His way of giving man responsibility and of putting the question on his desk, saying, "You do it. You work it out." Who would want to live in a world where everything was done! Too much revelation, too much Divine intrusion would leave us without an occupation.

How often Jesus emphasized in His parables both the absence and the presence! The Kingdom of God is like a man taking a journey into a far country, calling his servants together and giving them the talents, saying, "You work it out." God is withdrawing Himself and giving man a choice and a chance to have dominion or destruction.

Some years ago, Dr. Arthur Compton of the University of Chicago looked at this hiddenness of God and discerned its meaning with clearer insight than the brave men who are now writing His obituaries. He expressed his belief that the Divine Father is gradually shifting control of this planet to the shoulders of His sons as fast as they can take it, just as any father must develop responsibility in his sons by giving them more and more of it to handle. That's what science means, he thinks; through these new insights century after century God is putting new power in man's hand and new light in his mind, compelling him to grow wise in the use of it and have dominion in the earth. That makes better sense than cynicism and it comes nearer to the message of the Gospel.

Finally, make your minds very still before the deepest question. Bring this hiddenness to focus on the mightiest event in human history—the revealing of God in the strange man of Galilee who was born in a stable and died on a cross. "Verily, thou art a God that hidest thyself."

I think men often look for God and do not find Him because He comes in such unlikely places and in such unexpected ways. Some scholars believe that the poignant touch in Samuel Beckett's play *Waiting for Godot* is the symbolic hint in it of the Christ story. Two common fellows were waiting for someone who never did show up; at least they didn't see him. They missed Him. They were looking for some big event, and were so expectant of a colorful, impressive Godot that they failed to recognize him when he came in common garb. Well, who looks for God in a stable, or hidden in humanity, or hanging on a cross? The people expected a king robed in glory, possessed of great power, and the majority missed Him when He came hidden in humanity. "Is not this the carpenter's son" (Matthew 13:55)? "Can anything good come out of Nazareth" (John 1:46, RSV)? They missed His mightiness in His lowliness.

That's precisely the story of the cross: they missed Him there, entirely. Some stood around in derision. "If you are the Son of God, come down" (Matthew 27:40 RSV). That kind of God they could understand—a God with power to command, a little king flexing his muscles or throwing his weight around. That's our kind of power. But a God who could love them, die for them, even while they were yet sinners, and also could pray for His enemies even as they smote Him, "Father, forgive" (Luke 23:34)—this was a God beyond their reach and still quite beyond ours. How often we look for Him in the wrong places and do not recognize Him when He comes!

Every so often I like to call to mind the life of the Japanese Christian, Toyohiko Kagawa, who spent years of his life in the slums of Kobe. He was a little man without much of a body; one lung was gone through tuberculosis. Doctors here in America told him he couldn't live, so he went back to Japan and said, "If my life is short, it will be full." He went into the slums of Kobe, got a little room where the needy people could get to him, and there in the stench of the back streets he *lived*. One day he went out in the streets to preach as usual. With a small group of people around him, he took his favorite text, the love of God. It wasn't an easy place to preach the love of God—a dismal street, dreary day, sleet and rain falling at intervals to disperse his congregation, and rough men laughing at

56

him. "The little man," they said, "and his funny talk about the love of God! What does he know about God, or what does anyone know whether God loves or not?" It seemed they had the right side of the argument, for even as he tried to answer them he coughed (a hacking cough), spitting up blood. And they laughed again, now partly through pity. "If God loves," said one, "why doesn't He do something for you? A small wind would blow you over." But the persistent little man lifted his arm, wiped blood from his mouth with his sleeve and went right on with the story about the great love of God. Gradually, in the cold street, their raucous voices got still—for stealing in on even their pagan minds was the realization that right there before their eyes was the proof of what he was saying. A little man was standing in the cold spitting blood and yet loving them enough to be standing there doing it.

"Oh, that I knew where I might find Him." Look for Him not in the glittering show: look for Him in the common things around you: look for Him in the laughter and sorrow and sacrifice of people you live with. Look for Him in the struggle for justice, in the courage of ordinary men and in the redemptive forces healing the hurts of life. Above all you'll find Him hidden in humanity, this God-man who said, "He that hath seen me hath seen the Father" (John 14:9), and of whom it was said, "Though he was rich, yet for your sakes he became poor, that ye through his poverty might be rich" (II Corinthians 8:9).

The Christian church today is in a mood of deep introspection, and I guess we're all coming to see a little more

57

clearly that if we are to move the world even an inch
nearer to God, we must identify ourselves with it, get
down into the mess and make men feel through our compassion.

4

Outside the Temple

ACTS *9:1–5, 23–27*

HERE IS A BIT of history which has often been repeated.
The newly converted Saul of Tarsus came up to Jerusalem
to join with the followers of Christ, whom he had only
recently persecuted; and they, fearing him, shut the door
against him and refused to admit him, or even to give
him a hearing. Luke says that they were all afraid of him,
not believing he was a disciple. It is rather amusing now
to remember that in that first century the man who did
most to expand the Christian enterprise, the Apostle Paul,
was at the beginning shut out of the church, feared and
cold-shouldered by both its followers and leaders. How
often and in how many ways it has happened since!

Dr. Halford Luccock had a sermon on "The Church's
Fear of Allies." "The fear of the church," he said, "has
often led it to reject assets of immeasurable worth." We
are confronted today with a question that may hold in it
the same open-end dilemma. Is secularism an enemy or
an ally? Is it something to be feared, shut out, or is it to

be nourished as a potential expression of God's larger purpose? That's one of the big questions floating in the air today.

Take a moment, now, to define terms. It is a good idea when we talk about something to start with some working knowledge of what we are talking about. What is secularism? A few years ago we knew, or thought we knew, what was meant by secularism. It is a word made prominent by a man named Holyoke in the middle of the nineteenth century. Some trace it farther back to the seventeenth century, when it had no overtones of religious hostility but was a neutral word used to distinguish between the political affairs and religious affairs, between the church and state, between what was sacred and what was profane —a word which originally meant "outside the temple." All that went on inside the church was sacred, and belonged to God; all human activity outside the temple— business, politics, government and everything that had no religious significance—was secular.

It is interesting to see words change their meanings and take on new shades of meaning as they move through time. In the nineteenth century Holyoke was an atheist. He organized a society of secularists composed of atheists and agnostics who had no use for religion and whose creed was simply a belief in this world only. So the word has come down to us with two shades of meaning, one the dictionary definition, pertaining to this world only, this present life; the other has definite overtones of religious antagonism. In our time, secularism has been generally condemned as an evil, and as an enemy of religion.

Rufus Jones, the Quaker, wrote a document in which

he said that the real rival of Christianity in the world today is not other religions but secularism, a way of life that does not recognize God as essential to it. *Life* magazine, in a strong Easter editorial in the early fifties, claimed that the real enemy of Christianity today is not other creeds but secularism. Georgia Harkness, a Methodist theologian, wrote a whole book on it. The first sentence is, "Christianity's major rival in the Western world is secularism," which she defined as "the organization of human life as if God did not exist." Just a few years ago we had it pinned: we knew what we meant by secularism. We *knew* it was an enemy of religion, this organization of life as if God did not exist.

But today the world has changed, the climate has changed and strong voices in the church and out of it are calling us to take a new look at the word. *Is* God confined in His love and concern to that which goes on within the walls of the sacred institution, the church? Or is He at work "outside the temple"? Does this secular world with its vast activity, complexity and technology belong to God or to the devil? Is secularism enemy or ally? A whole new theology is growing up around that question, and some believe that for the next two decades most of our theology and religious thought will be concerned with it, and with the relationship between Christianity and the big, wide, booming world.

Some of the theology is far-out, radical and unstable —too ambiguous to last, too abstract to understand—and a bit off the beam, like the lopsided house a realtor was trying to sell to a customer. When the wife of the customer pointed out that the house was lopsided, he said, "Of course it leans a little now, but just wait till we get the paint and plaster on her; then she'll stand up straight enough." We have a lot of lopsided theology today, which is unfinished, and a lot of odd terms that confuse. They are not yet thought out, and even with paint and plaster they will not stand up.

We do not have to get fouled up with far-out theology, religionless religion, worldly Christianity, and so on. If you knew it *all* you would still be half-witted, but the main thrust of the emphasis is important. The argument is that the church is in trouble today partly because it has lived too much in isolation and is preoccupied with itself and with its institutions. There must be a turning toward the world, a deeper involvement of the church in the life of the world. After all, God loved the *world*, not just the church, and we too must love the world, not just stand off and condemn it but identify ourselves with all its strivings.

There is more of God in secularism than we know. It is not the unmixed evil some churchmen have thought, and it is not the unmixed good some humanists have thought. It is a strange mixture of both, and when we forget that, both the church and the world are in trouble. The church has often alienated some very creative minds, and is still alienating many fine young minds by its isolation, its assumption that only through the channels of the sacred church does God's revelation come. Often, it has seemed to disown some things its own vitality has produced and shut the door against seeming enemies who might have been its allies. If that is what is meant by "a turning to the world," we had better give it a hearing.

Take it first in the content of our culture. In this mixture we call secularism, there is more of God than we know. No one today would dispute the historical fact that much of our western culture had its roots in Biblical religion, in both Old Testament and New. From three streams has our civilization come—Roman law, Greek culture and Hebrew religion. In the interweaving of these strains Western Europe shaped its life. Thus out of the ferment of the Old World, which was in religious ferment, the New World was settled. Here in America we are so used to a society permeated by a thousand years of Christian teaching that it is difficult to know what is secular and what is not. We have to be accurate here, and not claim too much; for what we have in the western world is not Christian civilization but a strange mixture of many cultures, good and bad. Nonetheless it would be impossible to write an honest history of western life apart from its Biblical rootage, the permeating influence of Christian ideas—so much so that if a person wanted to get away from Christian influence he would have a hard time finding a place to live. Go through the country some time. You would think we had a Hebrew invasion because so many of our rivers, mountains, cities and people have Bible names! Our city is St. Petersburg, the burg or village of St. Peter. Our secular society is literally saturated with Christian concepts and even Christian names.

Certainly our institutions of mercy and compassion were spiritually motivated. With the coming of Christianity, a whole new outflow of charity widened out across European life in the quickened consciences of men and women who had caught the spirit of the Great Physician. The healing of the sick, the care of orphans and the poor

—all of it was first done haphazardly and unskillfully within the church. Now, fortunately, much of it is taken over by secular institutions, by agencies outside the temple and supported by the state; skilled, trained people are doing a better job in social service than the church could ever do with amateur and voluntary service.

As with institutions of mercy, so with institutions of the mind. In the Old World the universities came out of the monasteries. Religion and education were one. The first university on American soil, Harvard, was built to train men for the ministry. In colonial America, if you didn't want religious education, you had *none*. That was all there was. Go down the list of great universities: Chicago, Princeton, Brown, Notre Dame, Duke, Vanderbilt, Emory, Yale, Dartmouth, Columbia, Boston, Illinois, Pennsylvania—out of the first 114 colleges founded east of the Mississippi, 104 were established by some branch of the Christian church. Religion and education—one!

Today, in a pluralistic society, education has become more and more secularized, outside the temple and divorced from religion—so much so that it has reached an almost ridiculous absurdity in which children can't legally say prayers in a public school. (Although I heard that in a Fort Lauderdale, Florida, high school the seniors put up a sign, DON'T WORRY. AS LONG AS THERE ARE FINAL EXAMS THERE WILL BE PRAYER IN PUBLIC SCHOOLS.) So charged today is the secular climate that even in church-related colleges some students picket the administration, protesting chapel or any distinctive Christian procedure that might violate the students' right to an *unbiased* education. Stephen Leacock, the Canadian humorist, said he had found the sure cure for campus problems is to abolish the student body. Since all the problems take rise in the student body, Mr. Leacock believes we should eliminate the students and let the professors go around lecturing to each other. Education, we say, is now secularized, outside the temple.

Does anyone think of democracy as the expression of religious conviction? Hitler did. Karl Marx did. They were experts in democracy. They had no illusions about the source of it. If we have forgotten how democracy was born, the Communists have not. Karl Marx said that this democratic concept of man, the idea that man has value and rights as an individual, is the illusion of Jewish-Christian beliefs. There is more of God in our culture than we have dreamed! The secular is not wholly secular; it is shot through from top to bottom with Christian concern, conviction and revelation.

In the amazing outreach of the human mind, there has grown up something we call science. It has changed the face of the earth. Why do we so often speak disparagingly of secular science when there is no such thing as secular science? Is not the mind of man part of God's divine creation? Are not the laws of nature the laws of God? Is not any study of the world the study of God's world? Professor Hocking of Harvard called science the secular offspring of Christianity, by which he meant there is a parental relation here. It was the outgrowth of the religious strivings of the Middle Ages. Now what we are saying here is that there has been a constant interaction between the Christian movement and secular forces all through history, and in the interweaving there is no way now of untangling the threads. We cannot say this is from God or this is from man, or make a sharp distinction between them and tear asunder what God in His wisdom has joined together.

Two things are required. First, we who are inside the temple must expand our concept of the God who loved the whole world, and widen our thought to include the secular strivings of man as part of His saving purpose. God is working His will through the mind of man. It is a great mistake to shut God up in a church and to think of Him as utterly other, outside our common life and breaking in only when we stand in the temple and say our prayers. It is a great mistake to think of this whole enterprise of the mind outside the church as merely a secular event having no relation to the purpose of God, when it is God Himself who is the impulse for every creative deed. We need a bigger God than the God of the temple.

Those outside the temple must recover a sense of history and remember their origins, that there is a religious heritage in our culture which none of us can escape or disown. Secular men have been much too glib in dismissing God from His world. It is almost as though there were a conspiracy to get rid of the whole idea of God and to shut Him out of everything.

The Christian Advocate recently had a little story about a conference on church unity, in which a delegate said that it's the will of God that the churches come together. A crusty old newspaper man, a thoroughgoing secularist, hearing the name of God, perked up and asked how He horned in on this? Even in His church, sometimes, He isn't permitted to show His face. If the secular man would honestly analyze his own culture, he would say, like Jacob, "Surely the Lord is in this place; and I knew it not" (Genesis 28:16).

Now let us go on to heighten the matter a bit, maybe lighten it, by taking a good close look at some modern conclusions. There is a lot of good Christianity outside the church that does not know its name, having arrived at conclusions by trial and error and not yet baptized in the name of the Father, the Son and the Holy Ghost. I listened to a distinguished man from Chicago, the head of a multimillion dollar business there, address a class in sociology on the merits of sociology and its vision for the future. Sociology was his big word. Sociology does this, he said, sociology does that—all for the remaking of mankind. It was a good speech. After the lecture I thanked him and told him that every time he used the word *sociology* I put another label on it, CHRISTIAN SOCIAL CONCERN. He looked at me and said, "Who cares about labels?" I was properly squelched. Who cares about labels?

Sometimes the problem is sheer semantics, the substitution of one word for another word without divine connotation. Secular man says, "This is right." The religious man says, "It's the will of God"—same thing! Jesus said, "Our Father in heaven." Tillich said, "The ground of being." The prizefighter says, "The Man upstairs." Jane Russell, the Hollywood theologian, calls Him A Living Doll. Words? Labels? Symbols?

Someone said that Mendel's Law of Heredity is nothing but the affirmation of the Fifth Commandment. Sigmund Freud probed the human soul and came up with original sin, only he did not call it that. Psychiatrists trying to put

66

the soul together come up with the essence of conversion, only they do not call it that. They call it integration of personality, or the reorientation of the self—other words with the name left out.

Some freethinkers in Canada met in conference to determine what was really basic in human relations. They called it dialogue. Day after day they "dialogued" and finally came up with the conclusion that the one inescapable ethic in human relations is that every man must consider the well-being of the other man before he acts. But the whole thing flopped when someone said, "Shucks, that's nothing but the Golden Rule." Our modern age is full of these illustrations of how men outside the temple have been traveling by long roundabout journeys, on different paths, through trial and error, toward the same revelations inherent in the Gospel—and leaving out the Name.

Julian Huxley has been described as an atheist, but a deeply religious man in a godless sense of the word. The major virtues were defined as chastity, honesty, modesty, moderation, love and compassion. You almost suspect that Huxley had had his nose in the New Testament. These are the fruits of the Spirit.

There is a lot of good Christianity outside the temple that does not know its name; people unwittingly serve God and do God's work, even as they curse Him or ignore Him. After they have succeeded in being very shocking to some gentle old ladies, they turn out to be defenders of the Christian virtues—poets who would not be found dead in church, in their own modes of expression speaking truths identical with the theologians' truth;

novelists and playwrights, in spite of themselves preaching a segment of the Gospel, in their seamy, smelly, smutty plays, making us see and feel the brokenness and disorder of life when men are alienated from God and from each other. Some of us have a great affection for Albert Camus, who denied the reality of sin; yet in his book *The Fall* he pictured its reality better than any preacher. God outside the temple is speaking His word through men who never go to church to sing the hymns or say the prayers or pay up their church dues! God—outside the temple!

So here we have the church and the church outside the church, and the revelation given and the revelation going on through trial and error, moving toward a light. Certainly the time has gone when we can claim we have nothing outside the church but irreligion and nothing inside but the pure and undefiled. The lines today are badly blurred. We have people inside who do not know what Christianity is, who have very little Christian love and are sometimes full of bigotry. And we have millions of people outside, working earnestly toward Christian goals and groping toward a light and not knowing that it is the light of God.

What are we saying here? Are we reducing the Gospel to humanism, rubbing out the line between Christian and non-Christian? No. What we are saying is that the Kingdom of God is bigger than the church, that Christianity has grown faster than Christians and gone quite beyond its walls and deeper into the world's life than we know. Our mission is not to fear it or shut it out or condemn it, but to meet it squarely with a *no* or a *yes*. We must say no to its false pride, its hideous sin and its almost childish fallacy that human effort is enough. It is hard to believe in the sufficiency of man, the saviourhood of science and the unreality of sin in the midst of one of the bloodiest, messiest wars in human history accompanied by a tidal wave of violence and disorder. There is a secular terror as well as a secular hope. We can never be content to leave secularism unevangelized. Secular man (man without God) may build a secular city, but unless he has a changed heart and a bended knee to a higher sovereignty, it will never become a holy city.

But we also must meet it with a yes in its creative aspects, and recognize the manifestations of God's spirit as they break out in secular life, whether they come properly labeled or not. All good work is God's work. Wherever men seek the truth, God is at work. Wherever they seek justice, God is at work. Where two or three are gathered together for the healing or humanizing of life, there He is in the midst of them. The Lord is in His Holy Temple, but His Temple is wider than the walls of the church. There is great encouragement in the thought that we are not the only evangelists—life itself is an evangelist.

Teilhard de Chardin explained that there are times when we have a curious sense of standing at the edge of a great awakening, that something is trying to break through to us—even through a turmoil that will help the lovers of God and the lovers of men to recognize each other as allies, not enemies. God gets His will done through His willing servants who are consciously dedicated to it, but He also achieves His purpose through many unwitting servants who do not love or even know His name.

There is an interesting story about Thomas Edison. He had at the entrance of his home a heavy, clumsy gate. One of his friends often wondered about that gate and why a man like Edison would put up with such an unsightly thing on his property and one day he ventured to ask about it and to suggest tactfully that Edison find something more modern and easier to open or close. Mr. Edison looked at him with a twinkle in his eye. "Come," he said, "let me show you something." And he showed him how the big gate, through pulleys and ropes, was geared in with a pumping contraption. And he said, "You see, every man who comes to see me, no matter who he is—every man who opens this gate automatically pumps a gallon of water into a tank on my roof."

It is fatally easy to limit God to our little ways; we need to be reminded often of the broad sweep of His sovereignty, a sovereignty so wide that, as one of the great souls of the past said, "He makes even the wrath of men to praise Him." There are many instruments serving His purpose quite outside the churches. Every day the most unlikely people pass through God's gate and without intending it, often without knowing it, make some contribution to His purpose. This is what we mean by the Living God—the God who lives in history and acts.

Back in 1930, a discerning editor of a magazine said, "The children of the Kingdom are the friends of God, building with Him they know not clearly what—they have never fully known. Every unfolding of the divine

70

life within them and within history has been for them a surprise."

THE PREACHER'S MISTAKE

The parish priest
Of Austerity,
Climbed up in a high church steeple
To be nearer God,
So that he might hand
His word down to His people.

And in sermon script
He daily wrote
What he thought was sent from heaven,
And he dropped this down
On his people's heads
Two times one day in seven.

In his age God said,
"Come down and die!"
And he cried from the steeple,
"Where art Thou, Lord?"
And the Lord replied,
"Down here among my people."

BREWER MATTOCKS

5

Blunders, Bombers and Builders

I CHRONICLES *17:1–5, 22:5–11*

"I HAD IT IN my heart," said David, "to build a house to the name of the Lord my God. But the word of the Lord came to me, saying, You have shed much blood and have waged great wars; you shall not build a house to my name" (RSV).

Part of our current pessimism about the future grows out of our sure knowledge of human nature. How can we hope ever to make a better world than we have when we have nothing but human nature to make it with? Even if we could succeed through science and technology in making a perfect human society, human nature would corrupt it. As long as we go on being what we are, we shall go on having what we have. Someone has even put it in verse:

> We cannot have Utopia now;
> It's a waste of time to plan it.
> For if we had Utopia, how
> Would we find the men to man it?
> You cannot work the Utopian plan
> Unless you have the Utopian man.

So runs the talk and the deeper suspicion that doesn't get into talk. What about it? I think we'd better agree with it. In fact, it is precisely the premise from which the Christian faith starts out—the utter inability of natural man, of unchanged secular man, to enter the Kingdom of God or even see it. It will take better people than we are to make a better world than we have. New men—it will take new men, new minds and cleaner hands.

The Old Testament story makes a good picture of it. One day David the king sat in his grand new palace of Lebanon cedar thoughtfully reviewing the labor of his days. A sensitive man was David, a really great soul in spite of his glaring faults. As he sat there thinking, it came home to him that most of his life had been filled with fighting, and with subduing the national enemies. Though he was at heart a poet, the demands of his age had compelled him to be a warrior and to carve out for his people a living space. Most of his life he had spent in fighting.

Now at last had come peace. The kingdom was united, its enemies subdued and its life stabilized. What now? As he looked out from his palace on the national house of worship, he was humiliated. He saw only a dilapidated tent. That old tabernacle had been Israel's house of worship since the day of Moses—an old and battered tent. It didn't seem right. No house, not even the king's house, should be more beautiful than God's house. "Lo," he said, "I dwell in an house of cedars, but the ark of the covenant of the Lord remaineth under curtains." It is never right that we furnish our private homes with every convenience and leave God's work to be done in unsightly surroundings.

So in the mind of David there stirred a daring dream —to build a house, a worthy temple for the Lord. Immediately he sent for a preacher, Nathan the prophet. Wouldn't you like to have seen that preacher's face, or *any* preacher's face, when someone offered to build him a church? "Do all that is in your heart," said Nathan, "for God is with you." That's what any preacher would have said. But that night the prophet couldn't sleep. He was the kind of preacher who knew the difference between his own thoughts and the word of the Lord. The next morning he walked back to the palace reluctantly to tell David he would not be permitted to build that temple. It would be built, to be sure, but by other hands, by another generation. It could not be built by David's hands. Why? Let David say it. "I had in my heart to build a house to the name of the Lord my God. But the word of the Lord came to me, saying You have . . . waged great wars; you shall not build a house to my name."

David never complained about that disappointment, for with his sensitive soul he recognized a certain incongruity in the Temple of God—the House of Peace—being built by hands reddened with the blood of war. Solomon, the new king and the new generation, would build the temple; David the warrior and his generation would prepare the way.

This fine old story starts the mind moving in many directions. It is fascinating to study history and to see how different ages have called out different capacities in people and thereby exalted different types as the important men of the hour. The ages are not alike. We've had ages of faith, ages of reason, ages of discovery, ages of industry, and in each age a different man is exalted as the ideal, as the important man in society. For example, it is hard for us to grasp, in this very practical age, the fact that there ever was a time when the man whom we call an idealist was considered the important man. Yet we know that in ancient Greece the big man was the thinker, the philosopher. For long years in China the most honored man was the sage, the man of wisdom, the scholar. In the Middle Ages the big man was the architect, at least in that transition period when the gloomy Roman patterns were giving way to graceful Grecian lines, and the energies of the age were taking form in those mighty cathedrals.

In sixteenth century Italy it was the artist. Out of an age devoted to the fine arts came Michelangelo, Leonardo da Vinci and some of the greatest painters in history. In nineteenth century England the man of letters was exalted. It is doubtful if out of any age has come a more brilliant array of artists in human speech: Browning, Tennyson, Wordsworth, Thackeray, Dickens and a host of others. You may not believe this, but there have been spots where the preacher—the clergyman—was considered somebody. Every time someone jokingly calls me parson, something in my memory stirs in warm recollection of the day, long gone, when the men of my profession had some stature. For the term parson came out of the practice of referring to the clergyman, who in a day when there were few books was the one person in town who *had* books, as *the* person, or, in Middle English, the parson. He's not the parson now and likely never will be again.

Every age exalts its own ideal man. It is fascinating to follow that further, to study the cultural soils that produce the important person, the factors that call him out, that lift him up in one age and let him down in the next. If the age is intellectually hungry, the thinker will come up; if it is warlike, the soldier will be the hero; if it is torn by political conflict, the statesman will come to honor. Every new development, every change in the world's cultural pattern calls out a new kind of man to be the exalted one.

The world turned a corner one day when men wakened to the fact that it was round. And in the new surging enthusiasm for discovery the explorer, the pioneer or the frontiersman became the man. Rugged, romantic days they were, with men sailing the high seas. We are still hunting treasure from sunken Spanish ships off the coast of Florida. And I think the movies will never run out of Western pictures. Go West, young man, go West! The pioneer was the man.

Then, with the widening horizons of the New World and the simultaneous arrival of steam and power machinery, the world turned another corner. The pioneer faded out, and there was lifted up a whole new set of important men—the traders, the industrialists, the bankers, the businessmen and in due time the brain men, the scientists and technologists. These are the patron saints of our time, the big men our age has exalted. They have revolutionized the world. There has never been anything like it in history. Out of their brain and brawn and driving energy, they have erected on this planet a structure of material grandeur so without precedent or parallel that we have come to measure progress almost wholly in terms of their achievement. When we talk about progress that's what we mean—scientific, industrial progress.

They are not an unmixed blessing. They have left out too many things. By exalting the means of life out of all proportion to the ends, by concentrating the major energies of the age on wealth, on power, on business, on making things and on buying and selling them, they have created a materialistic culture stuffed with gadgets, machinery, tall buildings, congested cities—a big, booming, monstrous body and an undeveloped soul. The race has been standing still in artistic expression, in moral development, in philosophy, in theology, in political understanding, while it forges ahead in industrial and material advancement.

We must stop here and go back for a balancing word. There is a revolt today against mechanization, materialism and the big machine, but it is not likely to get too far; it is like Ruskin riding in a stagecoach across England to protest the steam engine. The clock of time will not be turned back, and we are not likely to park our brains in order to save our souls. God has no quarrel with matter. He invented it. And who says that materialism itself is a menace to man when it has given wings to his feet and power to his hands? It's a pious hypocrisy to bewail the materialism that has taken so much drudgery out of life. It's the lopsidedness we complain about—the big body, the little soul and its almost insane sense of values.

You get it in this: why should a manufacturer of

automobiles command a salary of a hundred thousand dollars or more while a teacher who trains the nation to think gets an average of seven thousand? The maker of machines, big—the maker of men, small! Our biggest awards go to the important men, those who minister to our material wants, our comfort, our convenience and even to our entertainment. You can see how we have exalted the entertainer. The funny man, the jester, the athlete and the entertainer have always had a place in society, often a worthy place. The man who won in the Olympic games in ancient Greece was an important man. Even the gladiator in old Rome was a hero—while he lasted. But in *our* society, where entertainment has become big business, a money-making device and a source of wealth, we've made our funny men and our athletes into minor millionaires. Fifty thousand is not too much for a good pro football coach, and the big stout fellows who buck the line earn more in a season than a college professor earns in a dozen years. *Time* magazine says that our top comedians' assets total five hundred million; so what we have is a pagan culture with big bodies and little souls. Out of its lopsidedness has come, as Toynbee has said, a world-wide unrest.

Out of this, there has been thrust up another man who always comes up in a troubled time—the soldier. He is not an unfamiliar figure by any means. He was the big man in the Roman Empire and periodically in all empires. He has been the national idol in Germany since the days of Bismarck. He was the first man in Japan for generations and the last man in China for just as long. But now suddenly he has become the big man everywhere, including

China. Take up your map: count up the nations in Africa, Europe, Asia, and Latin America in which the soldier or the military man is running the show! Forty percent of the world is under the soldier's hand. Out of the demands of an unsettled, revolutionary age has come the soldier to be the all-important man: the rest of us are important only as we hold up his hands and put new weapons in them. The only bad man is the man who will not fight. Some people think the twentieth century will be remembered as the hundred years' war. Certainly we have been a warring generation.

Where do we go from here? The important men of our time are the scientists, the industrialists, and the soldiers. Just before he left the White House, General Eisenhower, a soldier himself, warned against the danger of that combination—against the military-industrial complex. Where do we go from here?

That brings us around in full circle to the story of David and the question it raises. Who will shape the future? Who will be the important men of tomorrow? What sort of men are required now to build on this earth the House of Peace? The soldier? Can the soldier do it? Hardly! Grateful as we are for him, certain as we are that in times of trouble he will be around, no one in his right mind wants the soldier to be the big man forever, or wants the world to be an armed camp—least of all the soldier himself. What he fights to free men from is a regimented military world.

An air force chaplain in a bomber division, trying to cheer his men who had been in the thick of it, told them to remember that they were helping to build a new world. A young major in the outfit said, "You're wrong about that, Padre. We're not building a new world; we're just smashing up the old one." After the bomber must come the builder, and that means a new kind of man. The prophet told David he could not build the Temple of Peace. The demands of his age had compelled him to be a warrior and that made him unfit to be the builder. Winston Churchill said that, too, in his comment that the man who can win the war can seldom make the peace; but the man who can make the peace could not have won the war. And perhaps he was his own best illustration.

What sort of man does this age demand? That gets us into something very interesting—the striking similarity between the demands of the age and the promise of the Gospel. Both the demands of the age and the promise of the Gospel today are moving in the same direction. What sort of man?

For one thing he must be a changed man. The one illusion he cannot afford is to imagine he can stand still, remain unchanged, remain the same old man in a new age which science has thrust him into. The world around him has changed, and with it he must change. The scale and speed of it are beyond comprehension and impossible to keep up with.

As we come near the end of the second millenium—the year 2000 is just a generation away—thinkers all over the earth are trying to peer into the coming day and the shape of things to come, and while no prediction can be accurate, what they vision will alter out of all recognition the world of yesterday and today. He has certainly changed his world.

The great question is, Can man himself be changed? Can old habits be altered, old sins conquered to bring him up to date with his time? Can man himself be modernized? After Hiroshima, Norman Cousins wrote to the effect that modern man is obsolete. He is a misfit in a new world. He has leaped centuries ahead in making a new world, but he hasn't prepared himself to live in it. He's an old man in a new world. And now he has no option. He has changed the world so much, he must himself be changed to stay alive in it. The point here is that the demand of the age for changed men has always been implicit in the Gospel, and in the urgency of the changed heart and the new birth. That's what the church is for. That's what evangelism is. That's what Christ came to do—to change the world beginning with man himself! "If any one is in Christ, he is a new creation" (II Corinthians 5:17). Old things are sloughed off; all things become new. Both the Gospel and the age are calling for a changed man.

More than that, he must be an ethical man and a spiritual man; that is, he must open his mind to realities beyond the range of technical skills and scientific know-how. He must explore the meaning of things, and the purpose of human existence. We have grown up in a society in which the important man was the scientist. He was the man with the answers. He was lifted up by the demands of an age that wanted to know the *how* of things. He has been answering that in unbelievable ways, but the world has already gone beyond him. All the great questions have shifted from the *how* of things to the *why* of things. What's the use of knowing the *how* of things if we have no wisdom in the use of them? What's the use of knowing how to split the atom or to conquer the sky if it means the destruction of the earth? All the great questions now are ethical and theological—questions of meaning that science cannot answer and does not pretend to.

Dr. William Pollard, one of our top scientists believes that science will gradually take its place among the other disciplines as science is in its Golden Age. But golden ages do not last indefinitely. They rise, reach their peak, then become routine. Science now, he said, is on the rise. Religion seems in decline, but there's sure to be a renaissance in the religious dimension and in the great demand for meaning when these two shapers of life will go along together. Here again are the demand and the promise moving in the same direction.

Finally, the age demands a universal man. If anything has become clear in our time, it is the fact that the world has leaped far beyond the narrow horizons of the political mind, the mind that thinks in terms of sections, boundaries, empires or little red lines on a map. Geographically those little red lines have been erased. We're now six feet away from each other. That is the goal of the telephone engineers who want to link the world together so that anyone can talk to anyone anywhere, as though they were within six feet of each other. We cannot be old men in a new age in which all the problems are global, worldwide, universal, if we are six feet from each other.

"Gentlemen," Lord Shaftesbury used to say to his British colleagues, "you must study bigger maps." All the old maps are out of date: national sovereignty, white supremacy and the little red lines are as obsolete as the oxcart. The world has gone way beyond the little maps.

"God so loved the world." *That's* our map! Paul declared that in Christ there is no difference between Jew and Gentile, bond and free, male and female. We're six feet away from each other.

It seems a bit silly to say the church is losing ground and that Christ is a back number just when the world is beginning to be conscious of its planetary dimensions, and is reaching out for precisely those universals implicit in its message. "God so loved the world." What is coming on the earth? Nobody knows that. We know that potential disaster stands waiting in the wings. We must never be blind to the great darkness in human ways, but there's encouragement in the fact that so many things are on the side of hope. Pope John opened his little window for a little fresh air, when he opened the Vatican Council, knowing that the whole world is looking for a new forward step. Alfred Whitehead said the world is on the threshold of a creative advance, and Pierre de Chardin, that wonderful French paleontologist, said that we are moving into a painful crisis in the build-up of knowledge, and the pressure in human life will lead not to a breakdown, but to a breakthrough into a new order of mankind.

Let me close with a quotation from de Chardin. "Despite the wave of skepticism which seems to have swept away the hopes, . . . faith in the future is not dead in our hearts. Indeed, it is this faith [which is in our science and our religion] which must save us. . . . [More and more] I am convinced that this majestic process, which nothing can arrest, can achieve consummation, only in becoming Christianized."

So do not throw away your Bibles for awhile, and do not be too hasty in deserting your churches. We'll be around for awhile. The new age demands new men—that's our business. And it's at least the option of each of us to move under the hand of the living God in that direction.

6

Keep Moving

JOSHUA *1:1–7*

"MOSES MY SERVANT is dead; now therefore arise, go over this Jordan." Here is a bit of history about the God of history who has a purpose for nations, for people, and who through them is working out His purpose. It is a bit of history about people, too—people making history though they were not aware of it, making their way through a maze of peril and perplexity with a vague feeling of following a purpose larger than their own, yet standing for a moment bewildered, faltering on their path as folk have always done. Moses was dead. That was the dark, unbelievable calamity they had to face and come to terms with. Moses was dead. They had come to the end of a chapter, and some thought it was the end of the book.

Moses had been their George Washington. With a strong hand he had led them out to freedom and had somehow managed to forge them into something of a nation with a sense of going somewhere under the rulership of God. They had leaned heavily on Moses. They had never known another leader. They had turned to him in every moment of crisis, and the grand old man had never failed them. But now he was dead:

> By Nebo's lonely mountain,
> On this side Jordan's wave,
> In a vale in the land of Moab
> There lies a lonely grave.

That grave loomed up big enough to fill the whole earth. It stood up behind them like a great wall, closing off all roads to the past. There was no way back. Before them was the Jordan; beyond that lay the land of promise to be conquered. Just when they needed the strongest leadership, just when this new day was opening up before them, that one strong link with the past was broken. The only strength they had to lean on had collapsed. Some of them were terrified and wanted to go back, wishing they had never started. They had no heart for the struggle and the frightening uncertainties of the days ahead. And then, right in the midst of their consternation, there came this clear, commanding voice: "Moses . . . is dead; now therefore arise, go over this Jordan."

What a wonderful Book is the Bible, with its many parallels to so many events, happenings and experiences which every generation has to face. You need no word from me to emphasize the crisis nature of the time in which our lives are cast. To be sure, every age is an age of change, of transition, of something old dying and of something new being born. But so accelerated have the forces of change become that we are being told, and rightly so, that we are at one of the major turning points in history, on the edge of a new kind of age and at a place in human affairs that cannot be punctuated with a comma but requires a period: it is the turning page of a new chapter. The world has never before changed so widely and so deeply. Never before have so many turbulent forces converged at a single point in time. Never before have so many unsolved problems loomed up. What a fateful time we are now entering! We are in the midst of a far-flung revolution of unprecedented magnitude in which men everywhere are breaking with the past and clamoring wildly for something new.

Now to multitudes of people, the crisis time seems like the death of Moses to Israel—like nothing but calamity. It seems the end of all we have built up and trusted in, the breakdown of old beliefs and ideals and institutions and the collapse of what we have called civilization. The air is filled today with the same kind of consternation and the same kind of fear, uncertainty and bafflement that plunged the camp of Israel into gloom.

I have chosen this story not because it neatly answers our question—how could it?—but because it reminds us of a thought we don't consider enough. There is such a thing as the God of history, the living God who has a purpose for nations and for people; the world is in stronger hands than ours, and, therefore, what seems to us calamity is not wholly calamity. It is also opportunity. "Moses my servant is dead." Very well: get up, go on. Go across this Jordan.

86

Let us center our thoughts here a moment, because it is the heartening call of God to a nation's faith and courage. Let's remind ourselves first of all that this is the meaning of all change. There is a restless stimulus at the heart of the whole creation (call it by whatever name you wish) that keeps saying to everything in it: *get up. Go on.* Keep moving. Nothing is static in this world—nothing! Everything in God's universe is moving, changing, going somewhere. The world we live in is moving. Here we are, little earth men trying to get on another satellite, moving with incredible speed in four directions at once. All the giant worlds around us and above us are moving. Every particle of matter is changing. Heat and light are only waves in motion. Matter, which men once thought was stationary, is itself motion. The atom, once thought to be a fixed finality, is only a name for energy—something going somewhere. Such is the world we live in. Whichever way we look in it, whatever direction we turn in it, we find motion—restless, ceaseless, never-ending change.

Our bodies change. If you do not believe that, look at a photograph taken of you ten years ago. Cells that make up our bodies are no sooner built into the tissues than they begin to dissolve and die to make room for new material, so that we are changing physically with every passing day. A physicist said, "If you want to speak to me, you'd better hurry up because I'm changing every moment." And so, my friend, are you.

Our minds change. We smile today at what we believed yesterday. Our text books are no sooner born than they begin to die. Our homes change. We set up our little homes, put the chairs in order, get them all fixed up and time moves us on. The highchair—what's left of it—goes to the attic or to the Goodwill Industry, and in the dining room, before we know it, one chair after another is pulled back from the table and set against the wall. Like Jean Ingelow, we have to say:

> I had a nest full once,
> Oh happy, happy I;
> Right dearly I loved them,
> But when they were grown,
> They spread out their wings to fly

This is life, everywhere. Joseph E. Renan said that to him it was the saddest thing in the world that nothing would remain fixed, that everything was in flux, that nothing was good enough to last or keep. I suppose we have all had a tinge of that sadness, but we may as well get used to it, because change is only another word for life, and nothing we touch escapes it. It seems that nature is never so happy as when she is compelling man to move. A powerful, relentless stimulus is saying to everything: "Get up. Go on. Keep moving."

God has made this kind of world. His energies have gone into it. His mind is revealed in it. His purpose is being worked out in it. And that is what the crisis means. What we call *crisis* is nothing but the normal processes of change speeded up or abruptly focused at one point. Life moves along smoothly for a while, like the action of a slow motion picture, then suddenly it gets speeded up. Forces that were building up for a long time come to climax. Events fall in rapid succession, and our emotions are jolted and wrenched by the dislocation of sudden upheaval and swift change.

"Moses is dead!" It happens like that—suddenly. We look at something that cannot be true, yet is true. The crisis is an hour when something like an earthquake shakes our foundations, and what we have trusted in, leaned upon, taken for granted, seems to collapse, and we are out there on our own like a little bird flung out of its nest, compelled to summon new resources. It is often a terrifying hour. We do not like it. We would much rather things would go along smoothly, as we had planned them to go. In fact, we so dread the dislocation of swift change, the demands of the crisis hour, that we have fallen into the habit of calling it a time of hardship. We ought to quit that. I mean we ought to quit resenting the crisis time, because what we are really resenting is growth. There may be exceptions to this. Undoubtedly there are, but generally speaking the hour of crisis is the hour of growth—the time of opportunity when the mind is shaken and stretched into new dimensions. It is the living God asking something new of us, moving us against our inclinations into situations where we must grow up, go on or go under. Such, I say, is the crisis hour. It brings us to a moment when we must change or *move*.

There were people in Joshua's day who did not like that. There they were, part of a movement—a movement in which God was leading them out, a movement which all generations since have remembered as one of the most meaningful moments in history—the Exodus. And the only contribution they could bring to it was to stand around grumbling about the hardships and sighing for good old days that would never come again. I suppose we could say it is human nature to do that. We seldom see the creative moment when we are standing in it.

There were people like that in the American Revolution, in the age of the Renaissance and during the Reformation. They saw nothing but calamity and the collapse of old things. There they were with their hands on the most creative moments in generations, times when freedom was being hammered out on the anvil of human anguish and when history was moving in a dynamic, new direction. And all they knew was that they were in a heap of trouble, having a hard time. So clear is history about this point that one is tempted to say that the most likely place to find opportunity is smack in the middle of trouble —not in the smooth, easy days, but in times of crisis, when all things are upset and we have to move. New ideas break though, new standards emerge and new vitalities crack up through old crusts to take shape in human affairs.

What a wonderful Book is the Bible! It tells us much about the time of crisis, when the living God speaks to man and says to him: "Move on." The Book of Joshua opens in the midst of a crisis. He needed this word from heaven, and so do we. "Moses my servant is dead." Very well. That is not the occasion for complaint. It is the signal for a new advance. Get up. Go on. "Go over this Jordan."

I am making no glib predictions of the future. I do not know what is coming on this earth. No amiable angel has whispered that secret to me. I am saying only what our faith has taught us, that God has made this kind of world with change in it as part of His creative purpose. This is the meaning of change. This is the meaning of the crisis hour, with the living God saying to everything, including man: "Get up. Go on. Move forward." He is saying that in the very construction of our bodies. Had you thought of that? When God fashioned man He made him to go only in one direction; there is no provision for retreat. He has eyes not in the back of his head, but in the front; he has hands to tackle the task in front of him; he has feet faced only in one direction. There are no weapons in the back, no tools to reshape the past, no provisions for retreat. He is saying in the very construction of our bodies: "Get up. Go on. Move forward."

Let us go on to remind ourselves that this is what He is saying to the church. Here is the church of the living God set down in the midst of a revolutionary time, called to bear witness in a generation moving swiftly and breaking with the past. What is the mission of the church in a time of swirling change? A lot of hard and earnest thinking is going on about this, because what is going to matter most in the years ahead is the quality of mind, the measure of faith and the grasp of divine purpose we can bring to it. There is abundant evidence that the church as we know it must undergo deep change and mobilize its people for a new kind of thinking. It is not united enough, nor Christian enough, nor resilient enough, to match the new shape the world is taking. There is a strong tendency in the church toward stuffy conservatism, to get itself identified with the unchanging past. In the minds of many forward-looking people now (people concerned about the world), the church seems an out-dated institution.

It seems to them a relic of a by-gone age, clinging to old customs, encrusted with old traditions, and in many lands linked with the forces of reaction and identified with old systems which are doomed shortly to pass away.

I tell you, the church is notoriously slow to move. If you do not believe that, you try changing something in the church, or try building a church that does not look like every other church. Have you heard the jingle about the dachshund? The dachshund, which someone described as a half a dog high and a dog and a half long, has to maintain long lines of communication. Senator T. V. Smith often quoted a verse about that:

> There was a dachshund once so long
> He hadn't any notion
> How long it took to notify
> His tail of an emotion;
> And so it happened while his eyes
> Were filled of woe and sadness,
> His little tail went wagging on
> Because of previous gladness.

It suggests the mood and the mind, in the church as well as out of it. This is one of the stickiest impediments to the ongoing purpose of God in every age—people who live with their bodies in this age and their minds way back in another, facing the problems of today with the ideas and habits of yesterday. It was that mind, you remember, that blocked the purpose of Christ in the first century, and its tail is still wagging in the twentieth. The church has no business getting bogged down in the past. Of course there are some sound values in the conservative mind and much in the past that must be cherished and preserved, but when the church is true to the mind of Christ and to its own essential nature, it does not lead to conservatism. You cannot put Christ down among the conservatives. They killed Him because he was not. "Ye have heard that it was said . . . of old time . . . But I say unto you . . . go [further, move]" (Matthew 5:21–24).

Christianity differs from other religions in this. Among other things, it not only accepts change as a part of God's purpose for life, but demands it. That is what it is here to do—to change things, to change the world—and if in a time of change we have nothing but a wail, a nostalgia for old ways that can never come again, we are not prepared for the greatest demand our age is making upon us. Surely the lesson is clear. If we do not want radicals to change the world or to move it in directions in which we do not want to see it move, then we must provide some leadership, create a climate, provide a faith and be the forerunners of the new age that is trying through all the turmoil to be born.

Theodore Roosevelt once paid tribute to the old circuit riders, those preachers on horseback in early America. He summed up their contribution to the winning of the West when he said that they helped to keep alive the divine fire in the heart of the pioneers. This is the mission of the church in a time of change—to strike out across the Jordan, to pitch its tents alongside a changing, moving civilization, to keep alive the divine fire and faith in the

93

hearts of the pioneers, to be the way-show-ers of the on-going purpose of God. This is the call of God in the church. It belongs not to yesterday, but to tomorrow.

There was a final word that came to Joshua, and that above the raucous roar of change still comes to us. "Be strong and of a good courage." Be not dismayed. Be not afraid. ". . . as I was with Moses, so I will be with thee: I will not fail thee, nor forsake thee." I wonder if you see the broad, sweeping force of that. Moses is dead, but God is not. The past is behind you, but the God of history is before you. Whatever Moses had back there, we have, too. Whatever resources were available to him are still available to us. Generations may pass, conditions alter, faces change and leaders die, but the real leader of earth is, above all, change. "I will not fail thee, nor forsake thee." The God of yesterday will be the God of tomorrow, as mighty in the present as He was in the past. He needs only the kind of people He can use, men and women with their faces turned toward Him, people with faith and courage in their hearts.

What a grand text this is! I know that all of us have been interpreting this old story, each in our own way. Some of you have been giving it a far more personal application than I have emphasized, and it is right, of course, that you should. Some of you, perhaps, have been thinking not about Moses' grave, but about another grave beside which you yourself have stood, a grave that looms up big enough to fill your whole world. You are wonder-ing now, what about the Jordan? Some may have been thinking of other links with the past which have now been

94

broken, or the strength of some strong thing upon which you had leaned, now gone—collapsed. What terrific dislocations life brings to us! Whatever our application, isn't it a great word to carry into the time ahead? "Be strong and of a good courage . . . as I was with Moses, so I will be with thee: I will not fail thee, nor forsake thee."

This bit of verse is not particularly related to the subject, but I like it because it is a kind of antidote to two extremes which are much with us: on the one hand cynicism which thinks nothing can be done, and on the other hand, sweetness and light that leave it all for God to do.

A tired old doctor died today, and a baby was
    born,
A little, new soul that was pink and frail, and a
    soul that was brave but worn;
And halfway here and halfway there,
On a white, high hill of shining air,
They met and passed, and paused to speak in the
    flushed and hearty dawn.

The old man looked down at the soft, small thing
    with wise and weary eyes,
And the little chap stared back at him with
    startled, scared surmise;
And he shook his downy head:
I think I won't be born, he said,
You are too gray and sad. He shrank from the
    pathway down the skies.

But the tired old doctor roused once more at the
      battle-cry of birth,
And there was memory in his look of grief and
      toil and mirth;
"Go on," he said, "it's good, it's bad,
 It's hard, but go on, it's yours, my lad";
And he stood and urged him out of sight, down
      to the waiting earth.

Who said we were to have an easy time here? Did Christ
ever say that? Does the God of the Bible promise it? "Only
be thou strong and very courageous. [As I was in your
yesterdays, so I will be in your tomorrows.] I will not fail
thee, nor forsake thee."

7

On a Clear Day
You Can See Forever

MATTHEW *4:1–11*

ONE DAY IN THE village the carpenter laid down his tools
for the last time, closed the door and walked through the
outskirts of the village up the winding path into the hills.
Far into the night he walked, until he found himself
among the caves and rocks of the wilderness with the cry
of the wild beasts in his ears. He had to go there: he was

96

impelled to go. "Then was Jesus led up of the spirit into the wilderness to be tempted of the devil."

What does this story mean to us, this account of the Son of Man tempted by the devil? We may never wholly know, but we have come far enough to know that the temptation of Jesus was a mental conflict He endured in thinking out His plan of action. He had come to be the Saviour of mankind and the answer to the prophets' hopes, to bring salvation in. To suppose it was merely the temptation of a good man to be selfish, to do an evil thing, is to miss the point. Every man's temptation must be interpreted in the light of his life purpose. Jesus' purpose was the Kingdom of God, to change the hearts of men, to bring them to God. That was the end purpose of His life, and the conflict in the wilderness concerns the means by which He might reach that end and achieve His purpose. We know also that He must Himself have told this story to His disciples, describing His spiritual wrestlings in these simple pictures which they could remember, even if they could not understand.

If we had seen the temptation, we would have seen no devil, no temple in the distance: but just a young man alone there with His thoughts, day after day wrestling with Himself—wrestling with the issues, thinking them through, seeing the shortcuts and tempted to take them and spurn the alluring ways that could deflect Him. And finally with His mind made up, clear-eyed and certain about the method which must be unflinchingly followed, He came out of the wilderness with quiet and calm in His soul, and angels ministered unto Him. We need to remember He was no longhaired, holy prophet. He was a strong young man of thirty, the clearest thinker with the most realistic mind the human race has known.

Dostoevski, that powerful Russian mind, was quite sure there was nothing in literature to compare with this for insight. If it had been lost, not all the wise men of the world could have restored it, for it gathers up in pictorial speech a whole epoch of human history—the invisible encounter between the forces of good and evil, between the truth about life and the secular lie, upon which so much of our civilization is built. From the record we can trace the movement of His mind as one plan after another suggested itself.

How could He win the world, change the hearts of men and bring them to God?

Every minister should be permitted occasionally to give credit to his wife. It was Florence, my wife, who suggested to me—in fact insisted—that sometime I should preach on the temptations of Jesus and under the title of a play then running in New York, *On a Clear Day You Can See Forever*. Neither of us knew what the play was about, but that title is magnificent, *On a Clear Day You Can See Forever*.

Here in the desert long ago our Lord fought out a battle and with clear perception saw forever—clear through the problems of life that still perplex and bedevil the world.

It began with bread. Almost everything does, so basic is bread to life. "Command that these stones be made bread." Of course He was hungry: He had fasted many days. His eye fastened on the small smooth stones of the desert which travelers say look very much like little loaves of bread, and an idea which He called a temptation took shape there in His mind. Bread—that's a good place to start. Poverty, hunger—feed people and they'll follow. They'll follow anyone who will give them bread. That's how every politician gets his votes and how every ruler rises to power. Feed people and they'll follow. It is easy to see why Jesus should be tempted at this point, for He was no stranger to hunger. He knew what it meant to be poor. All His life He had seen the haunted look in the eyes of hungry people.

Studdert Kennedy has a vivid word about this: "He was surrounded, I believe by a innumerable phantom host of the world's hungry people. He saw them stretching out into . . . an endless sea. Mothers clasping puny children to their . . . shriveled breasts; fathers tearing open their ragged shirts to show the bones beneath their skin . . . while all around . . . like the moan of the sea there went up the cry . . . 'Bread! Bread! For God's sake give us Bread!'," This, He told His disciples later, was a temptation to Him.

"Answer that cry," the tempter said. "Anyone who can answer the cry of poverty can rule the world. If you are the Son of God, if you have God's power in your hands, use it to answer the real need—bread. How can you give them God if you don't give them bread? How can you make them good if you don't give them bread? Feed their bodies, and you'll get their souls. Never mind all that other stuff you want to teach them—God, love, brotherhood, *that* stuff. Who needs it? Give them what they need. Give them bread." There is a powerful plausibility in this, and, of course, some measure of truth. Millions still are bewitched by it. Whole ideologies have come into being around the idea that since man is animal and little more, bread is the thing. That is all life is when you take the trimmings off—a hard, grim battle for bread.

The Communists have launched a world program on this basis, the application of man's total energy to his materialistic needs. Never mind God; there is no one there anyway. "Not prayer," said Karl Marx, "but plows, steam shovels, tractors. Feed the people, and they'll eat out of your hand."

The business world is obsessed with it. The business of life is business; everything else is trimming—culture, religion, even morals. Seek first what you shall eat and drink, what you shall put on, and people will be good and other things will be added. Even the church, every so often, gets sidetracked in its legitimate concern for social needs and loses sight of the higher spiritual dimensions, and social service becomes religion. But Jesus rejected this line of thought, sensitive as He was to the physical needs of man. He was no dreamy Hindu thinking men could live without bread. At the center of His prayer was "Give us this day our daily bread." But He saw farther than Karl Marx. On a clear day you can see forever.

There in the wilderness He saw, with penetrating insight, clear through the problem of the world's bread. He saw that it could not be solved by bread alone, that it was everlastingly rooted in the spiritual, that there was no solution without getting the evil out of men's hearts and no solution apart from some other things. He said, "Man shall not live by bread alone, but by every word that proceedeth out of the mouth of God." The need for other words He saw two thousand years ago.

100

It is becoming a bit clearer to us now. We must learn some other words, or no bread. *Conservation* is one such word, which is just another word for stewardship, the care of the earth which is the Lord's. If we continue to blight the earth and waste its resources, we'll have no bread for all these teeming millions coming on. *Work* is another. God has ordained that man shall earn his bread with his sweat and his toil. You do not help people by feeding them or housing them *unless you do a good deal more*. They will take your bread, gobble it up, lie down, go to sleep in the sun and be no different and no better. But give them other words; give them hope, faith and self-respect as children of God and they will stand on their own feet and take care of their own bread. *Love* is another word. Laugh as we will at *brotherhood*, it is getting clearer now that without it we shall have no bread. If we quarrel over bread and fight each other to get it, we shall destroy it, the world and ourselves with it. This is no theological battle fought out there in the wilderness; it goes right to the heart of the modern world's number one problem—the problem of bread. Every day it gets clearer what Jesus told the devil in the desert—that man cannot live, cannot survive by bread alone, but by every word that comes from the mouth of God.

"Very well," said the devil, "there are other ways. There's a legend among the people that when the Saviour comes, the Messiah, He will come floating in the clouds, descending in power and great glory upon the temple. What about that? Give the people a sign. Advertise yourself, throw your weight around, let them know who you are. Show them your credentials. Cast yourself down into their wondering midst. That is exactly the kind of magic they're looking for. People are as hungry for sensation as they are for bread. You won't get far as just a carpenter with nothing but the truth in your hand, especially your kind of truth, this 'Blessed are the meek.' They won't go for that. But a miracle, a spectacular miracle, undeniable proof, that will get them. They'll follow you anywhere if you will give them proof. Advertise your alliance with the Almighty. Give them a sign—jump." And this, Jesus told His disciples later, was a temptation to Him.

Are we surprised that He was tempted to impress the people with His power? Everyone is. And why not? If to make people good, if to win them for God a convincing miracle is needed, why not? Why not make use of their credulity to serve His righteous purpose? Why take the long way around striving with men's hearts, if by a turn of His hand, a shortcut, He could storm their hearts and win their allegiance right away by a dazzling demonstration of His miracles? "Cast yourself down." He must have wrestled with this alluring possibility a long time.

What would *we* have done if we had all power in our hands? I imagine we would throw our weight around and let people know who is who and what is what. But He rejected it; having heard in it the voice of the devil, He set it aside as useless to His long-term purpose. On a clear day you can see forever, and now we can see it, too, at least in part, after years of Christian history. Here in the wilderness, centuries before His time, His clear-eyed moral insight went right to the roots of one of the world's oldest and most degrading evils—superstition, credulity and the temptation of people to put their trust in magical religion.

There are only two kinds of religion—magical and moral. You can trace them all through history. One looks to God to do things *for* us, the other looks to Him to do things *in* us and *through* us. Put this down and remember it. There was no disposition in Christ to leave men helpless, infantile and undeveloped, and to do for them what they must do within themselves. Magical religion does not make people good. It may excite their wonder, but it does not change their hearts or make them better: it leaves them where they are. It often makes them worse, producing the very opposite of goodness, encouraging them to look to God or government to do for them what they must do for themselves if they are to rise up to be His sons. And perhaps the worst punishment God could visit upon us would be to answer all our prayers, to break through by miraculous intervention, heal all our diseases, solve all our problems and leave us children, undeveloped. All through His ministry He was pestered with the question, "Give us a sign," and often He was depressed to see crowds around Him goggle-eyed with wonder at His miracles of compassion, while they blithely brushed off the moral meaning of His message. He did not come to be a miracle man: He came to bring people to God.

This world has always been a pushover for magical religion. The church itself has been cursed with it—with shrines, good-luck charms and hocus-pocus. What a mixture the church has been in spots, with goodness and superstition coming along together! There is heartening evidence today that the Roman Catholic Church, which has been the source of so much good in the world yet not unmixed with evil, is beginning to purge itself of the kind of superstition that Jesus repudiated in the desert and the kind of supermagic that feeds the hungry for sensation and leaves men no better than they were. It is a persistent evil: throw it out the door—it comes back through the window.

So Jesus rejected the shortcuts, both bread *and* magic. He thrust them aside as useless to His purpose, and then went on to face the most tempting of all temptations, power—political and military power—by far the most common foundation upon which all the kingdoms of the world are, and always have been, built. The devil took Him to a high mountain and showed Him the kingdoms of the world.

During those first sad and frightening days of World War II, the President of the United States tried unsuccessfully to keep Italy out of the war and to keep Mussolini from lining up with Hitler. The President telephoned Mr. Churchill and said that it was no use because somebody had taken Mussolini to a high mountain and shown him the kingdoms of the world.

Think of all the ambitious men who have stood on that mountain looking down on the kingdoms, wanting to rule the world: Alexander, Caesar, Napoleon, Hitler—and none of them with an ambition as far-reaching as that of this man in the desert, this Son of Man with God in His eyes. He saw stretched out before Him the kingdoms of this world and the glory of them. He wanted with all the passion of His soul to win them for God and to make them subject to God's will. "Pray then like this . . . Thy kingdom come, Thy will be done, On earth . . ." (Matthew 6:9, RSV). He wanted the world!

"Very well," said the voice, "you can have it with just a little sidestepping." The devil knows at lot about kingdoms: he has been mixed up in them for a long time. He pretty much gets his way with them. "But you see," he said, "what you have to do to get them. These kingdoms are mine. They don't go much for God-talk. They follow me. They're mine." The devil is almost truthful at times. (Mark Twain said he would very much like to meet the devil, because anyone who could hold the complete allegiance of nine-tenths of the world's population for so long a time must be a highly interesting and fascinating person.) "They're mine," he said. "But I'll make a bargain with you. Worship me a little, take my way, use my power to get them. You have the right purpose. I have the right weapons. Let's make a deal. You haven't a chance, you know, with your kind of power, righteousness, justice, love and brotherhood. They won't go for that. You'll get yourself killed with that. The odds are all stacked against you. Don't be a fool. But a throne, a crown on your head, a sword in your hand, a little of *my* kind of power—let's make a deal, pull together, and the end will justify the means."

Now just how much this was a temptation to Jesus we can only guess. All through His ministry there were those who wanted to make Him king and who wanted to put a sword in His hand and have Him take the way of power. But how much there in the wilderness, He thought of force as a way to achieve righteous ends, we do not know.

From our knowledge of Him today it seems rather unthinkable that He would even consider it, but there was nothing in that day to make it unthinkable. To Mohammed it was not unthinkable. To millions of Christ's own followers it has not seemed unthinkable. Think of the Holy Wars, of the conquests under the church flag, of the Crusades marching out to kill in the name of Christ. It was not unthinkable then, with Romans everywhere. It was that kind of world. We only know that He rejected it. He did not believe that the end justifies the means. On a clear day you can see forever.

Two thousand years before the atom bomb, He saw clear through the ultimate suicide of naked force. He saw with clear-eyed perception the light that is beginning to dawn on us, the utter futility of animal force to serve divine ends or even human ends. Some people think that God is using the atom bomb now to make us see that we must find other ways of getting along with people, other ways of dealing with our enemies. Nothing is clearer now than the limitations of force, the weakness of the sword. They that take it perish by it.

These are the principles He hammered out, there in the wilderness. We often wonder what these people mean who think of the religion of Christ as visionary—a lovely story for the children, a beautiful sentiment, God, mother, home and heaven. The way of Christ is the way of life to which men must turn somewhere, someday, to find the path to their social hopes. "It is written," He said. "Thou shalt worship the Lord thy God, and him only shalt thou serve." If you're going to come out where God is, you

106

have to take God's way to get there. On a clear day, on a clear day you can see forever.

8

The Lure of the Infinite

ROMANS *8:18–23*

ONE OF THE STRANGE but undeniable facts about human beings is that there is something within us which apparently the other animals do not share—an upward slant of the soul, a restless endlessness of desire. It was never said more picturesquely than in Kipling's poem, *The Explorer.*

"There's no sense of going further—it's the edge
of cultivation."
So they said, and I believed it—broke my land
and sowed my crop—
Built my barns and strung my fences in the little
border station
Tucked away below the foothills where the
trails run out and stop:

Till a voice, as bad as Conscience, rang interminable changes
On one everlasting Whisper day and night
repeated—so:

"Something hidden. Go and find it. Go and look
behind the Ranges—
Something lost behind the Ranges. Lost and
waiting for you. Go!"

Behind these exciting words is an exciting fact. There
is an upward slant in the soul of man, an everlasting
whisper, a universal, urgent pressure toward the infinite.
He is born with an unquenchable desire. He cannot be
content with what he knows, what he does, what he is,
what he has. Everlastingly he is lured on by what his
imagination pictures beyond the ranges. And when he
reaches it, when he catches up with his dreams, he proceeds to dream still further. Granted, there are other
elements in human nature not so good, but right here let
us rejoice in this one. The lure of the infinite is in man; a
restless urge to reach the more that lies beyond.

What is it that man wants? What is he reaching for? If
you were to sit down and try to put that yearning into
language, I imagine you would have trouble with it, for
language itself is like the thing it attempts to describe: it
is a reaching for the impossible. What word, what combination of words would you use to define the ultimate
goal of man's perpetual quest? Have we any word or
phrase big enough and good enough to say it? Many books
have been written on this. All sorts of people—preachers,
poets, politicians—have talked about the Holy Grail, the
Fountain of Youth, the New Republic, Utopia, the Great
Society, the Beloved Community and perhaps half a
hundred others. We need better words than these. They
are not big enough or good enough. They are themselves

just little signals pointing to the infinite thing we are after. What is its name?

Do you remember Henry van Dyke's story, *The Lost Word*? The hero in it wanted to put out of his mind all thoughts of the divine, to banish from his mind even the name of God, but he found that when he wanted to express his gratitude or his need or even his highest aspiration he had no word to say it. He perished for lack of a word. Our world today is very much like that. There is enormous activity in it, deep searching and great hopes, but we have no word to say it. We don't even know its name.

Let us follow that through history. Let us start off mildly by remembering that it is this mystery urge within which is the basic motivation of everything that we have called progress.

Dr. Frank Boreham of Australia once wrote a book with the title *The Other Side of the Hill*. He said that was the oldest question in the world: What's on the other side of the hill? Wherever you find a man you will find him looking toward horizons. In the cool of the evening —that is, in his highest moments—he is looking to where the hilltops break the skyline, muttering to himself, "I wonder, I wonder what is on the other side of that hill?" Dr. Boreham went on to say that this is how history and geography came to be. The first man looked out to the distant hills and wondered, just wondered, but his sons and his grandsons climbed them. They went beyond them, east and west and north and south they went. Losing touch with the old home, they climbed one range, then another; settled in this valley, and then in that valley, and so tribes and races and nations and empires came to be. The other side of the hill, that's what did it—the charm of the unknown, the everlasting whisper in man's soul.

Some of the impulse moves toward discovery. Columbus heard the whisper, heard it above the ridicule and laughter of men, day and night repeated in his brain: something hidden—go and find it. And he followed the whisper across wastes of water to a new and undiscovered world. A secret is an exasperating thing. It teases and taunts and tantalizes. "Twinkle, twinkle, little star, how I wonder what you are." Out of that came astronomy. I suppose the Tower of Babel was the forerunner of our Palomar Observatory, and the same impulse in the men who built it is itching now in the spacemen. There is no mountain peak so high on the earth, no wilderness so desolate, but that some man has felt the urge in him to conquer it. "Because it's there," said George Mallory, when he explained why he wanted to climb the big mountain. (Although in Tennessee some hillbillies say that's why we go round it, because it's there!)

It is precisely this same lure which has produced our scientific age. If there were no secrets, there would be no science. Man chafes under his limitations, is not satisfied with himself, cannot see far enough with his eyes, cannot hear far enough with his ears, cannot travel fast enough with his feet and cannot get enough done with his hands, so out of his driving dissatisfaction he dreams up these amazing tools and mechanical contrivances to extend his powers and multiply his energy. The lure of the infinite!

Part of the urge moves toward excellence in achievement: something in his nervous system will not let man

110

be satisfied with anything short of the perfect. We never finish anything. We never arrive. Do a good job today and you have to do another tomorrow. Preach a good sermon this week, and you have to get up and do it again next week, and do it better. There is no end to anything: perfection is always one step beyond. Some people work in electronic plants where they measure space to the billionth of an inch, moving toward perfection. At UCLA they are developing a torch to produce a temperature of a hundred thousand Fahrenheit, ten times that of the surface of the sun.

The urge is in the athlete. Bob Hayes, once the fastest human being in the world, ran a hundred yards in 9.1 seconds. He wanted to make it in 9. Why? Who knows? The lure of what lies beyond! It is in the artist too. When Thorwaldsen was asked, "What is your greatest statue?" he said, "The next one." It is said that Chopin, the composer, used to walk the floor chewing his quill pen to pieces, tearing up his half-finished scores. Why? Because he couldn't make music good enough to please the people? No, because he couldn't make it good enough to please himself.

One night after an organ concert at Pasadena Community Church, some of us went up into the chancel to see what was left of the organ after Virgil Fox got through with it. Imagine a man practicing here two days and then again from 10 o'clock to 2 in the morning. What was he after? Perfection. He didn't quite reach it, but that was the goal. Jesus described it in talking about the kind of righteousness we must reach for. "Be ye . . . perfect, even as your Father which is in heaven is perfect"

(Matthew 5:48). That is the goal, the purpose of life. Of course we never reach it; we pursue it, and that, itself, is the purpose.

Some of the pressure moves toward better ways of getting the world's work done. Right now a compelling mandate is in man's soul to improve his world, to find better solutions, to. rethink his modes of living and behavior. The whisper comes not only from the mountains and the wastelands but also from the still, sad music of humanity. A doctor hears the whisper and follows it beyond the ranges to find the cause of cancer, the cure of polio, the secret of better health. A lawyer is attracted by the possibility of a finer ethic, some better way of handling juvenile delinquency than putting kids in prison. People picket in the streets to dramatize social injustice and create a more sensitive social conscience. Young men and women, thousands of them, strike out for Africa or South America to help create a better way of life for people living in the shadows. Ask them why they go; they cannot tell you. A whisper, a voice as bad as conscience, says, "Find something." They cannot say quite what.

Our generation is full of this enormous search for better answers because our world is in deep trouble, for something not found yet—the secret ways of brotherhood and justice. The nations are close together but have not learned to love. And it is amazing how some powerful hand in history keeps maneuvering us into situations where we have to think new thoughts and find better answers for increasingly complex problems.

Former Dean Robert Russell Wicks of Princeton, following this mystery urge through life, said, "We are bound together in an infinite procedure in which every end is but a beginning, every solution but an open door to new problems on a higher level, every truth a challenge of more truth to be known, and all improvement but a hint of more than has entered into the mind of man to conceive." The lure of the infinite!

If you're going to get a word to describe this, you will have to get a great word. No small word will do. All this work, this human enterprise, this enormous searching— what is it moving to? What is its ultimate goal?

Now we have come far enough along, in all this, to consider a further fact. So universal is this lure in life, so relentless is its pressure, so pervasive is it in all mankind that we are quite convinced that it rises from a source other than ourselves. The whisper in man's soul is higher than any human whisper.

You may remember the story of Professor Osborne of Oberlin who saw a small country boy holding a kite string and following it, although the kite itself had gone so high he couldn't see it any more. Asked how he knew the kite was there, he said, "I feel the pull of it."

If you are ever tempted to doubt the reality of God in your lives, or the presence of God in our history, ask yourself the question, What is this mystery urge that runs like a living spirit through the whole human race, disturbing us, calling us, keeping us aware of larger possibilities, leaving us dissatisfied with the highest heights we have climbed and the best we have attained? This vague unrest is not of human making. We did not invent it. In fact, we are often conscious of resisting it. How often has the whisper come to you, calling you to get up and

113

be something better than you are, and you did not like it? You asked to be let alone. You were content to string your little fences in the foothills. You made adjustment.

In youth I set my goal farther than the eye could see.
I am nearer to it now—have I moved it nearer me.

REBECCA MC CANN

In many ways that is a terrible word—adjustment! And that is why we are not better Christians than we are.

How often the church, too, has been deaf to the voice, when for long periods of time the trails ran out and stopped. It was content with its settled creeds and stately cathedrals while the world rushed by it until in some turbulent man, a Martin Luther or a John Wesley, came again the everlasting whisper, and it was up across the ranges again where the Spirit of God was moving in some new venture and toward a better answer.

The whole world sometimes gets sluggish and settles down in fatal ruts and stagnant forms: nations and great empires live in the foothills of privilege, hoping that nothing will disturb the way things are and dreading those awful whirlwinds of change that shake down their institutions and scatter the people like chaff. It won't do. Something here won't permit it. We are under the rule of a living God dead set on righteousness, whom someone described as the relentless enemy of everything but the best. What difference if we call Him by other names? We say ambition stirs men, necessity drives them. We talk about duty, honor, self-respect; but these are only other

114

names, words and attributes of the Greater Mind, of whose creative power our small energies are but the dim reflection.

> Like tides on a crescent sea-beach,
> When the moon is new and thin,
> Into our hearts high yearnings
> Come welling and surging in;
> Come from the mystic ocean
> Whose rim no foot has trod,—
> Some of us call it Longing.
> And others call it God.

WILLIAM HERBERT CARRUTH

Now we come to this. We started out to find a word for it, or a phrase or a figure of speech, big enough to name the restless search of man, high enough to define its goal and comprehensive enough to gather up its divergent longings and put a sense of unity into our fragmented life. There is really no secret about it: it is not even unfamiliar. Jesus called it The Kingdom of God, and even then He was borrowing an old word long sacred to His people. What a pity we have let the word drop out of our common speech when it was the most common word in His! "The kingdom of God," He said, "is within you" (Luke 17:21).

Here is the clue to the complex book of life. Here is the place where the pathways of men converge. Here is the lost word that gives meaning to the sum total of human hopes. Here is what the whole world is really groping for, though we may not know its name. Just as those exploring parties deep in South America, searching out the headwaters of the Amazon and each groping along his appointed path, came one day within hailing distance of each other, then at last to the open and infinite sea, so there is a oneness in the search of men and a center where they meet and understand each other. The explorer mapping out his bit of land; the scientist finding something hidden behind the ranges of the known; the inventor putting little bits of metal together; the poets, artists, musicians and teachers, with their little scraps of truth and beauty; the missionary bringing light to darkened minds—these are people, all of them, who have heard a whisper. They followed the lure of a light within; and, while their paths seem divergent, consciously or unconsciously they were linked together in one supreme enterprise, the outlines of which they could see only dimly and the final goal of which they could not see at all: they could only feel the pull of it.

This was the faith of the prophets. They believed, indeed, they were *obsessed* with the faith that the Living God was at work in history and moving toward a purpose, the final end of which was always, to them, on the other side of the hill. This was the faith of Christ, too. "My Father worketh hitherto, and I work" (John 5:17). He listened, and out in the world of men and things He heard the sound of work, and it was God's work. The Apostle Paul took it up. "We then, as workers together with Him . . . (II Corinthians 6:1). The whole creation groaneth and travaileth . . . (Romans 8:22) waiteth for the manifestation of the sons of God" (Romans 8:19).

There is an ancient heathen legend that tells of a day

when men stood up before the gods, daring to be like them. They knew that the gods had something extra, a god-spark, and they wanted that spark too so that they could walk more proudly in the earth. But the gods were jealous of these men creatures, the legend goes on to say, and they kept the spark. They tried to hide it from men. Weeks, months and years went by and they could not find a hiding place, for men were inquisitive creatures. They ranged the mountains, plumbed the seas and peered inquiringly into the heavens, and there was no place where the divine spark was safe from men, until one day the great god, Brahm, stood up before the gods and signaled in the long hall for silence. There was a smile of triumph on his face. "Fear not," he said to his fellow gods, "for I have found the place. I have hidden the spark. I have hidden it where men never in all their lives will think to search. I have hidden it deep within their hearts."

This is the glory of our faith: Jesus never tried to hide that spark from men, because He wanted them to find it. He wanted them to know it. He wanted them to be born of God, to find the secret, to see the glory in it and to stand up straighter because of it. "The kingdom of God," He said one day to some very ordinary people, "The kingdom of God is within you" (Luke 17:21). And that is at once the reason and the final goal of man's holy discontent.

9

What the World is Waiting For

ROMANS *8:1–23*

"FOR THE CREATION waits with eager longing for the revealing of the sons of God" (RSV). The man who wrote that was trying to say a tremendous thing which, perhaps, cannot be put in words. He was trying to picture this earth as a living thing yearning for something to happen to it, to give it life and personality, to make it speak and feel and groan as if in childbirth, to look longingly down the road for someone's coming. On first thought, it seems to be fantasy, like a Walt Disney cartoon; but the more we look at life, the more we learn about its mysteries, the more we realize that Paul is trying here to express a reality that is perhaps beyond the range of words.

Words are clumsy things. When we try to express our deepest thoughts, the best we can do is to make little pictures, or symbols, or metaphors. This is a metaphor, and behind the metaphor is the suggestion that this old world, rough and unfinished from the hand of God, has within it a deep urge for completion, and is waiting with eager longing to be peopled with a race of godlike men and women who will tackle it, mold it and fashion a soul for it after the will and spirit of its Creator. That, I say, is a tremendous thought.

Even to ordinary people like ourselves, there come some intimations of the truth behind the metaphor. There is intelligence in nature, a bit of mind stuff in everything —so much so that when we speak of it we may call it Mother Nature. A tree is cut back in the garden and nature sets in motion an intricate process of healing. "Nature," we say, "takes care of it." In the accurate geometry of the beehive, in the instinct of the migratory bird, in the great reproductive urge that keeps life going everywhere, there piles up so much evidence of intelligence in nature that when we speak of it, we say Mother Nature, to give it life and personality with evidence of purpose in all living things.

Sciences comes along and carries the case much further: it makes the startling disclosure that matter itself is living. For a long time the brain men have been rubbing out the line between matter and energy, until nothing is solid any more. Even the electron in the invisible atom has no substance: it is only a convenient name for energy, or life, so that this whole creation from atom to star is held together by a vast network of invisible, living forces acting and grouping themselves together with an intelligence that is unbelievable. "All through the physical world," said one of our physicists, "there runs that unknown quantity that seems like the stuff of our own mind and consciousness." We can never get over the wonder of it.

It is this creation—orderly, living and mind-filled— that is yearning for something to happen to it and waiting for the sons of God to come. For with all its wonder, there is something terribly incomplete about creation. It is nature in the raw. It has come from the Creator's hand

119

rough, unfinished, like a great marble boulder from the quarry. Almost everything has to be done to it. God put the trees in the forest, the iron in the hills and the great reproductive urge in everything, but nature by itself cannot make the garden or put an orange grove on the hillside. Man must come to this rough and risky world with his brain and brawn and imagination, roll up his sleeves, clear out its rocks and stumps, harness its forces and beat it out with the sweat of his brow and the genius of his thought. In this old inescapable fact, this divine-human partnership, lies all the romance of living with creation waiting for the sons of God to come—waiting first of all to be discovered. Let us begin with that.

There is an old story of a Pennsylvania farmer who sold his farm because an ugly, oily scum in the creek made the water unfit for the cattle to drink. Years later he stood where an oil well had been drilled down into the creek bed, leaned up against a fence and sighed, "Ah, if I had only known." It is a prophetic story, for it is a parable from a much larger truth. This whole world is like that. It is a far more wonderful place than we have ever dreamed, rich in untouched resources as yet unknown. These are infinite powers hiding behind thin veils, waiting, as once this continent waited, for someone's coming. If these forces seem elusive, it is only because nature tells a man nothing he can learn for himself, for man himself must grow. Nature seems ready enough to yield up her secrets to those who seek and ask and knock; but sometimes nature throws out hints, or puts an oil slick on the water saying, "Come, dig down! Here it is." This has been the thrilling story of the modern world—the coming of the discoverers. Never has there been anything like it in history. They have gone up into the infinitely great, down into the infinitely tiny, and come back with little scraps of information in their hands. The thrill of discovery is part of the gladness of God, the shared joy of creation.

Edison said that we don't know a millionth part of 1 percent of anything. A millionth part of 1 percent—that is *ignorance*! The next hundred years, the next fifty, the next ten—what will they bring? Do you suppose God shivers in His shoes, afraid that we shall find the secrets? All creation is waiting with eager expectation to be discovered.

Let us go a little further now and say it is waiting also to be conquered. It is not enough to see it as an unfinished world: it is also a blemished creation, in some ways, with fierce forces lurking in its heart waiting to be subdued, mastered and controlled. It is a hostile world in many ways, full of forces that are heartless and merciless—so much so that someone thought there must be a conflict between the Creator and His creation. And some, looking at the cruelty, have lost faith in the goodness of God altogether.

Even in sunny Florida, where the weather is usually so mild that it does not bother our consciences to lie about it when it is not, even here an occasional tornado or hurricane blows in from the sea to remind us that nature in the raw is seldom mild. Hostile forces are here, and from the beginning man has had to battle against nature to go on living. Earthquakes shake down his little houses.

Frost, fire and flood crush him. Disease germs rise like soldiers from a million swamps. Huxley called it "a dismal cockpit." Darwin saw it as a grim, uneven battle in which only the strong can survive.

I once had a funeral service for a lovely young girl who tumbled from a path into a ditch swollen with a flash flood. She was an excellent swimmer, but the current was so powerful that it carried her into a drainage pipe. The pipe was blocked, or she would have been swept through it into a small pond, where she might have had a chance.

A grieving family might ask, "Is this the will of God, that a happy child should so lose her life? Must we only resign ourselves to this?" I do not know of anything that is less the will of God than that a child should drown like this. It is His will that we learn to conquer the forces of nature. There are laws here, stern laws, laws that we are gradually learning. We are here not to resign but to wrestle. This, too, is part of the glory of our time—the coming of the conquerors.

Mark Twain complained about the weather and said that nobody does anything about it. That is not exactly so. We have done a lot about the weather. We have learned to build a fire. Civilization followed the chimney. We have learned to blow clean cool air through a building when it is hot. (A Texan said the reason he did not like air conditioning was that it enabled the Yankees to stay south all the year round.) We have done a lot about disease, too: we have traced to their very boudoir these little bugs that knock us over. In a thousand ways and in a thousand fields men have been doing that—grappling with the unfinished, imperfect things to make something better come out of them.

Luther Burbank looked at a cactus, and said, "I don't like it," so he changed it. They have taken the old sour crab apple and made a Ben Davis. They have taken the old poison love apple and made a luscious tomato. They have taken the wild grasses and made wheat, barley, oats and rye. They have taken the old Yankee pumpkin and made a Georgia watermelon. Men have been doing that, driven by necessity but lured most of all by a deep instinct within them (which is part of the likeness of God in them). They have been grappling with the imperfect and conquering the forces that are hostile, and some of you will find the romance of living at this point. It is a great mistake to think of God as outside this process, to think of the awakening of the mind as a secular thing without divine meaning or purpose. All creation waits with eager longing for the conquerors to come.

We go now to the deepest fact, that creation waits with the eager expectation to be redeemed. This is the great unlearned lesson of our time, and we are all in a quandary now about how to lay hold on the redeeming forces that make humanity human. It is so easy to grow lyrical and enthusiastic about the awakening of the mind and about the new mastery of physical forces. We call going sixty miles an hour instead of six progress, until we ask, "Why? Where? To what end?" Then we remember what so much of it is used for and we see the whole enterprise of the mind bogged down in crass materialism, where even knowledge itself cannot get us anywhere worth getting, except to make the tools for faster life and swifter death.

Nobody is talking now about automatic progress, about every day in every way, getting better and better. Who is saying that now? Nobody! What if the sons of evil come? What if animal men, brain men and brawn men with no God in their hearts, with all humanity bleached out, should hold these powerful forces in their hands? We have had some glimpses of that. We saw it in the Nazis, in their scientific savagery; they were monster men with powerful forces—Dachau, Buchenwald. It sickened us; it frightened us. We have seen some hints of it in ourselves, under the veneer of civilization—Hiroshima, Nagasaki, Viet Nam. What if the sons of evil come? We cannot shrug this off or talk glibly about being emancipated from divine authority or from the old ethical rules by which civilization has emerged from the darkness. The problem of man is still that downward bent in his heart, by whatever name you want to call it.

Someone asked in a congressional hearing, "What progress are we making in militarizing outer space?" That is it! One man makes a discovery. Another man takes it, and with it makes a monster, threatening to destroy the very civilization that gave it root. Galileo, you remember, looked through curved glass. He was excited, too, thinking of what it would do for man, how it would push back man's horizons and help him to see. But then he showed his telescope to the senators of Florence; Alfred Noyes described those old men mumbling through their beards, "That glass will give us great advantage in time of war."

124

"O God of love:
Even amidst their wonder at Thy world,
Dazed with new beauty, gifted with new powers,
These old men dreamed of blood."

ALFRED NOYES

That is still the sordid, stubborn fact we have to deal with, and we cannot brush it off. We must face up to the irrationality of man, the frustration of knowledge itself and the terrific disproportion between the magnificence of the mind's adventure and the trivial, irrational and often immoral uses to which the discoveries have been put. If only a race of men would come with hearts to match their heads! How often we have thought that and said, "If only the sons of God would come." By far the greatest yearning of creation now is for the awakening and re-creation of the human spirit—for something to happen in the hearts of men to give them a spirit equal to their skills.

We yearn for this; yet every day our minds are bombarded with the emptiness and the futility of it all. We have a lot of tired novelists writing books on the nothingness of life. We are literally drenched with pessimism. If we wanted to be cynical, we have plenty of material, but we are not cynical.

We know there is no hope in nihilism. We want a faith. We want something to believe in. If we are looking for a faith to hold us now, to take the wobble out of living—a faith, an interpretation of life big enough to give meaning to the vast riddle and practical enough to give signifi-

125

cance to what we put our hands to—here it is. Perhaps this is the nearest expression to final truth ever spoken on our planet: *the whole creation is in travail, moving, waiting for the sons of God to come.* There is skin-deep optimism there, no shortcut Utopia, not even a God who can snap His fingers and get His will done in a hurry like the dictators, but just the long struggle in which we, with Him, wrestle to bring His purposes to birth. There is no pessimism, either. God has not abdicated to the Kremlin or to Washington, or even to join the brave men who are prematurely writing His obituaries. He is not absent from the world. He is patient, that is all, patient beyond all our understanding of that word. He keeps working toward His dream with undiscouragable hope, flinging out hints of what He wants—all sorts of hints saying, "Here it is. Come get it," and trusting with that huge faith of His that the truth will break through by and by, and that by the very light in His mind man will rise up to triumph in the spirit.

We should not feel sorry that we are born in a time of trouble, or go about with a we-who-are-about-to-die-salute-you attitude. Thoroughbreds have never talked that way. We must stand with these new tools in our hands and a bit of the light of God in our hearts and, be it ever so little, strike a blow for the emancipation of man to fashion a soul for creation.

Heinrich Heine, the German poet, had a story about a sculptor who was so skilled with his hands he could make anything that his mind conceived. One day he determined to make a man. He went into his studio, assembled the material and began his work. He fashioned a body first —a magnificent body—and placed on it a finely featured head. When he had almost completed it, the creature he had made spoke to him, "Master, give me a soul." It frightened the artist. He ran from the studio, slamming the door; but the creature followed him saying, "Master, give me a soul. You've made for me a magnificent body, now give me a soul."

This is the task of our time, and the whole world waits for it. Science has made the body, a magnificent body. Science has done its work well. I shall never vote for a moratorium on science until our morals catch up—as though we had to park our brains in order to save our souls. There should be no dualism in our thinking, no conflict between mind and heart. Thinking has not, will not, hurt us. It is only lopsided thinking related to one area of life. It is the application of intelligence to just one realm, which, after all, is just another form of ignorance that will hurt us. Science has done its work well; here is the body, and we have seen forces standing around it eager to give it a soul. Fascism has tried hard, and still tries, to give it a soul—an ugly, monstrous soul. The Communists have done their best and are still trying hard to give it a soul fashioned after the spirit of Karl Marx.

But we whose hope lies in the emancipation and not the regimentation of the human spirit, we know that the soul of creation must be fashioned after the will and spirit of Him who, when all power was in His hands, took a towel on His arm and became a servant and said, "The Son of man came not to be ministered unto, but to minister . . ."

(Matthew 20:28). To that spirit, to that great power dedicated to the service of the humane and compassionate heart, we consecrate and dedicate our lives.

10

The Seeking God

GENESIS *35:6–7;* LUKE *15:11–24*

I fled Him, down the nights and down the days;
   I fled Him down the arches of the years;
I fled Him down the labyrinthine ways
    Of my own mind; and in the mist of tears
I hid from Him, and under running laughter. . . .

From those strong Feet that followed, followed
   after.

FRANCIS THOMPSON

SEVENTY-FIVE YEARS ago, a Roman Catholic magazine in England published a poem by an unknown poet who but two years before had been a drunken, destitute drug addict. His name was Francis Thompson, and his poem was called "The Hound of Heaven." No one at the time thought it was much of a poem, or that it would ever have much of an audience. But it has been translated into more than sixty languages, and, as *The New York Times* said in an editorial, "It is one of the few English lyrics that make the same powerful appeal to all nationalities and faiths." Our own American poet, Robert Frost, as a young aspiring poet, found a copy of it in a Massachusetts book store and spent his carfare money to buy it. Eugene O'Neill, the playwright, memorized it: he knew every one of its hundred and eighty-three lines by heart. Some of its powerful phrases have become woven into our everyday speech. One phrase, "with deliberate speed," turned up in a Supreme Court decision. It has had a wide appeal, "The Hound of Heaven."

Basically it is a poem about the seeking God, His pursuit and final capture of the fleeing human soul, which is what the Bible is mostly about, from Genesis to Jesus. One of the first questions in the Bible is "[Adam], where art thou" (Genesis 3:9)? And its last page is a divine call to man: "The Spirit and the bride say, Come. And let him that heareth say, Come. And let him that is athirst come" (Revelations 22:17). The Bible is the story of a search.

We are quite familiar with the concept that puts the search on our side. We speak, often too glibly, about finding God, as though He were lost somewhere. And yet there is validity in the concept that the history of man is a search (often an unconscious search) for the living God. We could give multiple illustrations of people in all ages of time breaking through into awareness, discovery of a Presence too real to be denied. Plato had a myth that in the beginning man and woman were one person; then when they were separated—sundered in two—love became an appetite and a restless hunger urging them to be reunited. So in the heart of every human being is an unnamed hunger to be at one again with God.

The search for beauty is the search for God and the search for truth. Some find Him through suffering, through torment of inner emptiness or through some sense of need. Many have found Him through music, that mystic call of something beyond ourselves to something deep within ourselves. Some find Him through nature.

Something sacred whispers from the vaulted skies,
　　Something deathless looks from our homesick eyes.
And we are aware of something that runs,
　　From the heart of ourselves to the heart of the
　　　suns.

MARSHALL WINGFIELD

Not far away from us is God
As near as sunlight to the sod.
So near to the human heart is God.

Very real is the human search, and real, too, is the finding in many forms all the way from Ignatius, who said he found God while sitting by a stream watching its running water, to Billy Sunday, who in his own graphic way said, "I stumbled drunk into the Great Arms." So we can speak with a good deal of confidence about this, man's restless search. "The history of philosophy," said George Henry Luce, "is the history of man's long quest for God."

But certainly that does not cover the matter or even begin to reach the depths of the greater reality, the Divine quest for man. "[Adam], where art thou?" Adam was hiding, hiding in the trees; and it was said of the man Jacob that God was revealed to him when he was running away. That's what we have to deal with in our time: man not seeking but hiding, fleeing, trying to get away from the Holy One, and what's more, not making it. Strong feet following after! This is a more accurate picture of our restless generation. "I fled Him," said the poet, "I fled Him down the labyrinthine ways . . . down the nights and down the days . . ." with desperate haste, deliberate speed. What if this be the real truth about the plight of modern man, the secret of his feelings of futility and failure, the accelerated tempo of his culture, the tragic aspects of his life and his frantic attempt not to find but to flee, to get away, to hide himself from the eyes of the Holy One, and not make it?

Not easily does man get away from God or escape the inescapable. Always on his path are these strong Feet following, following after. You can name them: you can trace the search. The name of the first is *memory*—not the top-of-the-head kind but deep-down racial memory, hidden and half forgotten—the memory of an image stamped upon him from his birth. "Made a little lower than divine": he can never get away from that. "The life of every man," said Alan Richardson, "is full of pieces of unrecognized knowledge of God, intimations of his divine heredity which he has never learned to call by their proper names."

Macneile Dixon in his Gifford Lectures said that this is what the fine arts are—music, poetry, and painting— man's attempt to reach for and recapture the ideal, like some lost chord he's trying to get on the keys again, in remembrance of a perfection he once was given and must get back. Other animals aren't bothered with it. Like Whitman's cow, they chew their cud content, but man is tormented by it—by this something higher he must reach. He wanders restlessly like a traveler in an alien land in his artistic aspirations, hearing the echoes of his higher heredity and trying to get back the paradise he was designed by nature to inhabit.

Much is being said now about the rise of a secular man who is abandoning his old beliefs as though they had betrayed him. But the old beliefs have not abandoned him. They lie in the deep of his mind like a buried dream and they come to light in unexpected moments to surprise him. It's a bit like that very old story of the Russian girl who was brought up as an atheist. She had taken a government examination, and like all students she was worried about some of the answers she had given. One particular question in the exam had bothered her: What is the inscription on the Sarmian Wall? She had written the answer: Religion is the opiate of the people. But she wasn't sure, so she walked the seven miles to the Sarmian Wall to check it, and sure enough there it was: Religion is the opiate of the people. Greatly relieved, she forgot her ideology, blessed herself and said, "Thank God! I had it right." So even under the frozen ice cap of Soviet denial still stirs the dream, hidden and half remembered. That's why in Russia today there's a black market in religious pamphlets which the government is trying to suppress, and why, after fifty years of trying to kill the dream, common peasants are saying to their leaders, "You've buried

God no deeper than our hearts." Strong Feet following, following after—one of them is memory.

The name of another is *misery*—the misery of man against his grandeur, whether it comes in the form of anxiety, the sense of guilt, loneliness or emptiness or all that fills the soul with sadness in the sharp pain of estrangement. Strong Feet following! It's the age of anxiety. Men today are restless, lonesome, quarrelsome, alienated from God and from each other and homesick in their homes. We have moved from an attitude of sunny expectation to a dark mood of anxiety and frustration; and unlike our forefathers who looked for God through the order of nature, modern man is driven to seek Him through the disorder in himself. The air today is filled with voices complaining about the absence of God and the emptiness of life.

But what if the truth be the other way round? What if the sadness is a symptom of the hunger? It is odd that we should interpret it as a sign of Divine absence when it's the surest sign of His presence, the evidence from within of a love that follows and will not let us go. Anxiety is a signal of distress, of something wrong within that must be set right. A sense of guilt is the proof of our sonship. It's a sense of responsibility. If we could fill the earth with horror and feel no horror in ourselves, if we could walk out on our homes and our higher selves and feel no sense of guilt, our situation would be hopeless. Our misery is our hope. God put a sadness in the soul to call us back. When our lives are tangled and we feel fed up, we may think it is a sign that God has forsaken us, but it is the surest sign He's still striving in our hearts and will not let us feel at home when we are away from home.

"God," said Dr. Paul Tillich, "is present in the unknown force that makes us restless." As St. Augustine said long ago, "Thou hast made us for Thyself, O God, and restless are our hearts until they rest in Thee." Strong Feet, tracking you down!

More than that, God pursues man even in his *heresy*, through all those brilliant arguments against Him. We need to go a bit deeper into the plight of man and his flight from God to consider the real anatomy of atheism and why sensitive people rarely succeed in getting there. They may deny God, curse Him and cry out against Him, but they can never wholly ignore Him or escape Him or even get Him out of mind. This should mean something. Ask the question: Why is so much of our secular literature filled with God talk? Rebel poets, writers, dramatists are preoccupied with the tragic side of life, with the eclipse of God and the victimization of man and the revolt against religion. Why? If religion is finished, why not drop the whole subject and forget it? If God is dead, why don't they bury Him and be done with it? Why all this talk about God by men who don't believe in Him? We need to understand better that strange ambivalence in men that wants to kill the thing it loves and hate the thing that haunts it. How often we do things for reasons we ourselves don't understand!

Have you a teen-age daughter in your home who comes storming into the house after a quarrel with the only boy and saying, "Mother, if he calls I'm not at home. I never want to see him again," yet she stands there near the telephone waiting, hoping and praying for that ring? Through with him? Not yet, not quite.

I saw a cartoon in a newspaper of two pretty junior-high girls walking home from school, and Gregory was on the other side of the street. One nudged the other and said excitedly, "There's Gregory."

"Oh, we're not speaking any more. I've lost all interest in him. We haven't spoken for three days, six hours and twenty-three minutes."

How near is love to hate? Who knows?

A little girl, angry with her parents, ran out of the house after leaving a poison-pen letter. "Dear Mom: I hate you. I'm going away. Love, Linda." It's exceedingly difficult to know how much hunger is hidden in hostility and how often a man who calls himself an atheist is just a poor hungry frightened little man trying to hide his emptiness with loudness.

Or take the most militant atheist of our times, Jean Paul Sartre, the brilliant Frenchman. Why is he so pre-occupied with God? He tells us we must forget God—we're all finished with that; we must give up that search. Then he proceeds, in page after page of his plays and writings in his search for meaning, to shake his fist against the sky and justify his case against the Almighty. We must forget, he said. Then why can't he forget? He seems obsessed with the idea of God, haunted by Him. He cannot get Him out of his mind, and many intellectuals like him, despite their rebellion, are God-haunted men tormented by the Divine. They think they are finished with God, but apparently He is not finished with them. They can't get Him off their minds. Bishop Gerald Kennedy defined a Unitarian as a man who can't quite take it and can't quite leave it alone. The definition fits a lot of people.

Martin Luther understood this ambivalence, this hunger in the hate, and he said a bold and daring thing. "Nobody in this life," he said, "is nearer to God than those who deny Him. He has no children more dear to Him than those like Job and Jacob who wrestle with Him and cannot let Him go." You have to take high ground to understand this, for what he meant was that those who take God seriously enough to contend with Him are nearer to Him than those who take Him casually and in practical life ignore Him. Albert Camus understood this, too. *Time* magazine commented concerning his fellow intellectuals who had long ago left the church, that it was no news they have abandoned God. But some people wished they wouldn't spend so much time weeping on God's doorstep.

Edna St. Vincent Millay saw that touch of hunger in the hostility and wrote a discerning verse about it.

Man has never been the same since God died.
He has taken it very hard. Why, you'd think it
      was only yesterday,
The way he takes it.
Not that he says much, but he laughs much louder
      than he used to,
And he can't bear to be left alone even for a
      minute, and he can't
Sit still.

He gets along pretty well as long as it's daylight;
      he works very hard,
And he amuses himself very hard with the many
      cunning amusements
This clever age affords.

But it's all no use; the moment it begins to get
      dark, as soon as it's night,
He goes out and howls over the grave of God.

How do you get away? Where do you go when you hide? Not easily do we get away from God. He follows the hippies into the street—searching they don't know for what. And as Chad Walsh once said, "He stands behind the desk of the atheist as he writes his book to prove He doesn't exist."

The healing of His seamless dress
    Is by our beds of pain;
We touch Him in life's throng and press,
    And we are whole again.

Now let's get on to a conclusion. We've come far enough to see that the search is mostly on His side, not ours. We try to get away and we can't. Take the wings of the morning, fly to the ends of the earth, and He is there. Make our bed in hell, the hell of some sorrow or some stupid sin, and He is there in the misery that calls us back. Something greater than man is pursuing man, and because the world is round there's no place in it to hide; and because His love is great He will not let us get away. His goodness and mercy have followed us all the days of our lives. The old theologians had a word for this, prevenient grace. It means that God was long beforehand, long on the road before we were, and that we seek Him only because He first sought us. He is the searcher: we are the sought. How else explain the Gospel and the meaning of the cross, this man with God in His eyes, who said the shepherd was after the sheep, not the sheep after the shepherd? In one of our hymns we have caught the meaning.

> I sought the Lord, and afterward I knew
> He moved my soul to seek Him, seeking me;
> 'Twas not so much that I on Thee took hold,
> As Thou, dear Lord, on me.

How many men in the Bible were found by God while they were running away—Jonah, Jacob, Elijah, Saul of Tarsus on the road to Damascus? And the landscape along here is quite familiar. Francis Thompson wrote "The Hound of Heaven" out of his own experience and in it mirrored the experience of many.

Here in brief is a story of a man who died in 1963 but not before he left a deep impression on the skeptical mind of our age. He wrote thirty books, compiling an impressive defense of the Christian way. C. S. Lewis was an intellectual, a brilliantly witty scholar at Oxford and Cambridge and a convinced agnostic. He took pride in his independence and in his liberal thinking, and scorned religion as a refuge for the weak. "I had as little wish," he said, "to be in church as in the zoo." But then he was converted, and in a small book, *Surprised by Joy,* he told how he, like other intellectuals, was gradually, reluctantly brought back to faith in Christ by taking a good clear look at the alternatives. Little by little, he felt God closed in on him in spite of his resistance. "You must picture me alone in that room in Magdalen, night after night, feeling . . . [every moment] the steady unrelenting approach of Him whom I so earnestly desired not to meet. That which I greatly feared had at last come upon me. . . . I gave in, and admitted that God was God, and knelt and prayed: perhaps, that night, the most dejected and reluctant convert in all England. I did not then see what now is the most shining and obvious thing; the Divine humility which will accept a convert even on such terms. The Prodigal Son at least walked home on his own feet. But who can duly adore that Love which will open the high gates to a prodigal who is brought in kicking, struggling, resentful and darting his eyes in every direction for a chance to escape?" Strong Feet following, following after.

Of course, we must apply it to ourselves. Adam, where art thou? He's calling your name too. Where are you? Do you really believe that He is distant or absent, hard to find, hiding, or are we hiding from Him? He's nearer to us than we are to each other.

> Speak to Him for He heareth,
> And spirit with spirit can meet;
> Closer is He than breathing,
> Nearer than hands or feet.

11

That Muddy Old River

II KINGS *5:1–14*

"ARE NOT ABANA and Pharpar, rivers of Damascus, better than all the waters of Israel?" These are the words that almost blocked a miracle of healing and a movement of God's spirit in one man's life story long ago. Naaman! How wonderful is the Bible in making us see ourselves even in its incidental stories.

Naaman was a sick man. He was brilliant: he was successful, captain of the king's guard and a mighty man of valor. The record puts it bluntly: Naaman was a great man, *but* he was a leper, and every preacher looking for texts has been quick to seize on this one and to recognize its parallel.

Our age is like that; our civilization is like Naaman: great, mighty in many things, but sick with a sickness that goes deep. Like leprosy it holds on, and grows increasingly more apparent. Have you ever noticed that through almost every thoughtful analysis of our civilization there runs this continuous theme: great, mighty—*but*! Here it is in the preface of a book, a note so familiar we could have written it ourselves. "Never before have so many had it so good. No longer do we tremble in fear of hunger or hidden evils. The burden of killing toil has been lifted. Machines provide us with nearly all we need and much that we do not really need. We have inherited freedoms man has striven after for centuries. Because of all this we should be living in the dawn of a great promise, but now that we are freer to enjoy life we are filled with fear of the future, anxiety about ourselves, frustration and disappointment. For in the midst of our plenty, the meaning of life has eluded us." Pick up any book or magazine, and this is the inner theme: greatness in external grandeur, sickness at the center. So this old story of Naaman begins with an incredible aptness to the basic problems of our humanity. He was a great man, *but* he was a leper.

Let us stay with the story for a moment, because it has a most enlightening background. There was a witness in Syria, a young Jewish slave girl brought back captive from Samaria. As servant to Naaman's wife, she daily shared the increasing gloom which, despite the glamour of the king's court, had settled on Naaman's household. Her master was very sick. She remembered Elisha, the prophet in Israel, who sometimes healed folk. She ventured a suggestion to her mistress. The rumor reached the king, and while he had no particular liking for prophets and preachers, he encouraged Naaman, his chief servant, to go to Israel. At least it was worth the try. In fact, he said, "I will send a letter unto the king of Israel." Kings are like that. They have more trust in coercion than in persuasion. And so in a few days there rolled out of the city gate an impressive parade: Naaman, the national hero, chariots, horses, wagon loads of servants and bags of gold. Off he went to Israel with the confidence that there would be a cure. He had a letter in his hand to command it, money in his purse to buy it and a retinue of servants to impress everybody that he was worthy of it. He was a great man!

Then came the letdown and the disappointment. They did not pay much attention to him in Israel. First of all, the king down there got mad, being served with such an ultimatum as that. "Am I God," he said, "to . . . make alive?" He hustled Naaman off to Elisha, but the prophet did not roll out the red carpet either. He did not even come out of his house to greet him: he sent his servant. "Go and wash in Jordan seven times." Naaman did not like it. He did not like the reception, and he did not like the prescription. He was an exceptional man. He wanted exceptional treatment. (You know how it is. You walk into the office of the president of the company because you know him, and he, being busy, turns you over to a secretary who does not know how important you are!) "I thought," said Naaman, "He will surely come out to me, . . . call on . . . His God, and strike . . . the place." It is interesting to watch a man get mad, especially a great man used to giving orders. Here he was, Naaman, captain of the king's hosts, standing at the door of the Jewish prophet, his gifts despised, his magnificence ignored, and told by a Jewish servant to go wash himself in the Jordan. Of all rivers, the Jordan! That muddy old river! Up in his country they called the Jordan a ditch. There were better rivers in Syria. "Are not Abana and Pharpar, rivers of Damascus, better than all the waters of Israel?"

He was right. Mrs. Hamilton and I went by automobile from Jerusalem to Jericho to Damascus in a day. We crossed the Jordan near Jericho and thought of Naaman, for that is what it was, a muddy old river. But when we came to Damascus there were beautiful rivers, flowing fountains and sparkling waters, better than all the waters of Israel.

The great man almost missed it. He stalked off in a rage. He started back to Syria—mad. But he did not go far—there were the whiteness of his skin, the awful darts of pain and the ugly sores beginning to show through. He was a great man: he was captain of the king's hosts, *but* he was a leper. It was a servant who spoke common sense to him. "If the prophet had bid Thee do some great thing, wouldest thou not have done it? how much rather then, when he saith to thee, 'Wash, and be clean?'" When Naaman had cooled off and simmered down, he realized he had come to the right door but in the wrong attitude. He swallowed his pride, humbly went down to wash in the Jordan and came out of the river clean.

Now let me lift this out of an ancient time and set it in our own: let us concentrate on just one part of the story, on the other rivers, the rivers better than the Jordan. There is no broader hint in our time, which is now the subject of many books, than that our traditional faith, the Christian religion in which our lives were nourished, has lost its enchantment for modern men; and that the church has become irrelevant to modern life; and that religion itself, which some have called the "God idea," with its old-fashioned creeds and standards of morality, has outlived its usefulness; and that we must find now for this secular and sophisticated age a new language and deliverance. The spiritual history of our time could almost be written in terms of other rivers, of substitutes, of more sparkling rivers to wash in. And there is no sense shutting our eyes to the fact that in our impatience with old things and our fascination with things that are new, there has come a considerable diminishment of belief in the Christian solution to the problem of life and a widespread search for other ways of healing the sickness of the world. It is a kind of fatigue we are up against, a weariness with old things, old systems, old institutions and old standards. Christianity has been with us a long time, and it suffers the disadvantage of familiarity. We have heard it so often and for so long that we do not listen to it any more. The itch is on us for the new, the novel, the exotic and the spectacular.

This is a wonderful day for the cults. We have a rash of substitute religions, mostly from the East—old heresies updated, with none of the bothersome moral demands of Biblical religion and of Moses, the prophets, Jesus and that old stuff. Isn't it odd that here in the West we are reading Eastern books because we are looking for peace of mind? But in the East they are reading Western books because they want to wake up. A rash of exotic religions! Young people in our churches and on the college campus with a wonderful tolerance of all religions and with no understanding of their own, are almost pushovers for any religious fad provided it is labeled NEW.

A magazine published a vignette entitled "The Secret." "On Fifth Avenue during the Christmas rush," the reporter said, "I trailed a mother with a little girl about four years old. The little girl kept looking down with her eyes on the sidewalk. 'Why don't you look at the pretty windows, Gracie?'

'I'm looking for something,' Gracie said.

'What, for heaven's sake?'

'I'm looking for something to find.' "

Well, the whole secular world is like that now with its eyes fixed on the ground, looking down, not up; looking for something to find—for other rivers, more sparkling waters than the Jordan.

Some of the rivers are political. In modern Europe, the geographical center of what was once called Christendom, we have seen whole nations, once Christian, abandon the Christian faith, or what they call the God idea. Why bother with churches and creeds and confessions when chemistry is more powerful than Christ, and the strong man mightier than the Almighty? "Leave that old played-out Jewish myth," said Lenin. "Man himself is God and needs no father in heaven to rule his destiny." Other rivers, better rivers than the Jordan.

Some of the rivers are social. The hunger for God has not diminished: it has only been replaced. Social action has become the new religion for many—the cause, the picket line, the march, the demonstration in the street. Harvey Cox in his book *The Secular City*, said, "If you're looking for God today, you won't find Him in the churches. You will find Him in the World, out where the action is." His revelation is coming now through revolution and the struggle for social justice. Who can be patient with a religion that stays in church when the real struggle is out in the streets? Salvation by agitation—better rivers than the Jordan.

Some of the rivers are intellectual, sparkling waters of the mind fed by many streams. The crowding in of new knowledge has crowded out the old. The fascination of new gadgetry and the spectacular achievements of technology have captured the total attention and diverted the minds of men from all things theological and even philosophical. Why look to God for miracles when we can make our own? The research laboratory has become the new cathedral of man's hopes. Religion belongs to the dear, dead past—useful once, but who wants to listen now to an old story when we have so many exciting new options? Bonhoeffer said, "Man has learned to cope with all questions of importance without recourse to God . . . the world's coming of age." Salvation by diversion—better rivers than the Jordan.

We must take a moment to say that some of the rivers are very shallow, however sparkling the waters; they offer only a surface salvation. Listen to the TV advertisers, the hucksters of hope, the salesmen of salvation, full of promise of deliverance from all the ills of mortal life, all the way from loneliness to the fatigue of tired blood. It is an old superstition, this, updated and revised, practiced by medicine men clear back to ancient Egypt—something to swallow down or rub on to magically heal the sickness or at least to cover up the spots. It is some magic potion in a bottle to make you beautiful and get you a mate; it is a hairdo, a spray-on, a deodorant, a mouth wash to bring you out of loneliness into fellowship, to get you back where the people are. The advertisers are experts in sparkling waters and other rivers, appealing to unconscious hungers deeper than we know.

There was a French philosopher, Déscartes, who believed that every illness of the spirit was physically based, and therefore one day the cure for all our sickness and our sin would be found in medicine. We are having a fling at that. Millions now are turning to the pill bottle, as their ancestors turned to religion. Health authorities are alarmed at the growth of addiction and the assumption that every problem of life can be solved by putting something in the mouth—happy pills, memory pills, mood changing drugs, LSD (salvation by medication), pills to speed us up, pills to calm us down. To cure our collective headache we annually consume twenty million pounds of aspirin; we have doubled our intake in the last ten years, according to the Bureau of Statistics. And while we are slowing ourselves down with aspirin, we are zipping ourselves up with vitamins—twelve million pounds a year. Tallulah Bankhead, the actress, sat in a Philadelphia restaurant sipping a cocktail and popped a vitamin in her mouth. "All right," she said to her friend who looked at her with disapproval, "I like to build myself up while I tear myself down."

Imagine putting salvation in a pill or heaven in a bottle!

We quarrel only with the shallow assumption that it can be a substitute, and that every problem of life can be solved by putting something in the mouth. Salvation by medication! If the disease were only skin deep we would have it made.

Other rivers—some of them psychological. Here is some sparkling water to splash around in, new, exciting and full of hope: understanding the psyche, getting down to causes and inner conflicts, getting rid of guilt feelings, getting order into the disordered self. What need have we for creeds and confessions if the couch can be the church? In thirty years, said one confident disciple of Freud, there will be no churches or preachers, only clinics and psychotherapists. Here again, we have no disposition to quarrel with psychotherapy. The grace of God is at work wherever healing takes place. But I think we can say now without being unfair about the considerable gains of the psychological approach to life (because many skilled therapists deplore it, too), that too many people use it as a crutch. It appeals to human pride to learn that there are good, scientific explanations for guilt and failure and that we do not have to repent of anything, only ventilate and adjust. This is very palatable to people who are looking for something to find for a religionless religion. For we are not ordinary people: we are the enlightened people of the twentieth century. We are the exceptional people who need exceptional treatment, something modern, scientific and up-to-date. We can get our sins washed away without reference to God. Salvation by manipulation!

Here then are the modern rivers of salvation, better than all the waters of Israel. But with all our pleasant rivers here is our society still sick with the ugly sores showing through, crime increasing five times faster than population, messy wars breaking out, race riots, broken homes and anxieties increasing. We heal the rash in one spot and it breaks out in another, because the sickness is deeper than our wise men seem to know. Why has our age, so brilliant and mighty in so many ways, moved so much to the surface about the deeper meanings of life?

We talk about the renewal of the church, about a revival of our faith. When will it come? It will come when we Christians stop being apologetic about our faith, when we get certain again about its downright realism and when we understand that there can never be a substitute for the deep wisdom of the Gospel that calls all men to repentance, forgiveness and the transformation of the inner life. What can ever be a substitute for this? We are glad for everything that enlarges life, for the outreach of the mind and the promise of social justice. We are grateful for every new insight in psychotherapy, for every growing light in the dark corners of the soul and for every device that helps man understand himself and improve himself. I think we would rejoice if tomorrow some pill could be found to help the alcoholic in his desperate battle with the bottle, as insulin helps the diabetic and as a tranquilizer helps the emotionally disturbed. We do not know yet the mystery of body-mind, where sickness ends and sin begins. We have called many people sinful who were only sick, and we still send men to prison who should be sent to a clinic.

The science of health and healing has yet much to learn, and we are for everything that man can do to help man be whole and healthy in body and in spirit. What we do stubbornly protest is the shallow secular notion that improving the outside redeems the inside, that the external manipulation of body-mind can ever be a substitute for the deep wisdom of the Gospel. It may supplement but it can never supplant, for after the cures are in, after we have read the books, swallowed the pills and splashed around in the sparkling waters, there still remains something deep in every human life that we cannot manipulate away,—namely, a responsibility for life and an accountability to God. Go wash there and be clean! Can there ever be a substitute for the miracle of the changed heart? Or the magic of forgiveness of which this Old Testament story is a parable?

How often we talk about forgiveness as though it were old stuff, simple and commonplace. But I am sure that, if you had leprosy like Naaman and came out of the river clean, there would be a sound of gladness in your soul. This was the impulse in which the Christian church was born—*forgiveness*. The Greeks could never understand the gaiety and joyousness of the Christians: "We have redemption through his blood, even the forgiveness of sins" (Colossians 1:4). They fairly shouted that across the Roman world.

Every revival in history, every renewal of the church, had its beginning in that. We who are Methodists like to remind ourselves of the Wesleyan revival that changed the life of England, of those coal miners in the fields, the tears rolling down their grimy cheeks in the delightful discovery of forgiveness. Thumb through the hymnal sometime and see how many people are singing about that.

> He breaks the power of cancelled sin,
> He sets the prisoner free.

Do our new theologians really think that this is old stuff and out of touch with life? What a great lift would come to the world, what moral cleansing on its soul, if we could hear this word again and listen to what it means.

How does it happen? How does one become Christian, receive the grace, the cleansing of forgiveness? In Sunday school a teacher asked what we have to do before we can have forgiveness. One boy answered, "We have to sin." Most of us would have no difficulty in fulfilling that condition. Back in the private life of everyone is a restlessness that all our activity cannot hide. We are all candidates for this.

Pascal said that Christian life begins by dipping your finger in holy water. He was too big a man to mean that literally. What he meant was that you have to start somewhere, you have to take a first step. You do not become a Christian in your sleep. If you are too big to bend low, you will never make it. You have to begin somewhere, humbly, quietly, in some decisive act of commitment.

The second step is to accept the gift. By grace are you saved through faith, not of yourselves: it is the gift of God. If this seems old-fashioned, here is a quotation of a man who could hardly be called an evangelist of the sawdust trail, the late Paul Tillich. "In the midst of our futile attempts," he said, "to make ourselves worthy, in our despair about the . . . failure of these attempts, we are suddenly grasped by the certainty that we are forgiven, and the fire of love begins to burn. That is the greatest experience anyone can have . . . when it does happen, it . . . transforms everything."

I call you again to accept Christ, to take the gift. There are people whose whole future life could be determined here by your response to the calling of your name. In this moment of quiet to receive Him, take the step and remember, "As many as received him, to them gave he power to become the sons of God" (John 1:12).

12

Finding the Word

JOHN *1:1*

AN OLD PROVERB says that the dumbness in the eyes of animals is more touching than the speech of men, but the dumbness in the speech of men is more agonizing than the eyes of animals. Who has not often felt the dumbness in the speech of men—the weakness and incompetence of words?

Yet men have learned to speak words in nearly three thousand languages, tongues and dialects. They were the first human invention and are still the most magical things in the world. No machine that man has made, no modern wonder that has come from his hand or brain, is so mysteriously complicated as the mechanism of common speech. You wag a piece of red muscle between your jaws, set sound waves moving in the atmosphere and a small receiving set in your friend's ear, far more complicated than any radio, picks up your noises and, by a chemical miracle, translates them into meaning. The friend gets the thought or idea in his brain cells, like the one which passed through yours; then he answers back with a bunch of facial noises—meaning yes, or no, or please don't bother me.

It is mysterious business, speech; so, also, is writing. You sit down at a desk, make some queer marks and signs on a piece of paper, fold it up, and off it goes across thousands of miles to your Uncle Henry. When he puts on his bifocals and looks at your marks and signs, the chemical vibrations in his brain cells tell him what you want him to know—that you've run clear out of money, and will he please send some RSVP, PDQ.

The transmission of ideas through words! No mystery is greater than that. "In the beginning was the Word." In the beginning of everything—in the beginning of understanding, in the beginning of relationships, in the beginning of man's communication with man and God—was the Word. Man does not live by bread alone, he lives by words—by every word that comes from the mouth of God. All the things that get done in the world—good or bad—are done by words.

Fascinating, therefore, beyond all other studies, is the history of human speech—how words are born, how they got into the vocabulary, how a certain sound or sign somewhere in the past became the thought conveyer of a meaning, and then by common usage became the permanent symbol of thought. The story of language from the beginning of time has been the complicated process of finding the word, the right word, to fit the meaning.

There's a silly little story about Adam and Eve when they were given the task of naming the animals. Eve looked at one big, lumbering animal and said, "Let's call that one a hippopotamus." When Adam asked, "Why?" she said, "Because it looks like a hippopotamus." There is sense as well as nonsense in the story, because many words do have a psychological fitness in sound for the thing they describe: skunk, swish, rock, and so on. If you were to take up the dictionary, examine the words of our common speech and trace down their ancestral pedigrees, you would find some curious things in the woodpile of etymology.

A vehement man said, "By God, I won't," and vehement men became known as bigots, By-God men. The Roman charioteer used a sharp whip that cut into the flesh, the *sarx* of his horse; and from there on, bitter words were called *sarcasm*, words that cut into the flesh. In Virgil's day, a peasant built an inn at the place where three roads met—*Tri Via*. It was the *Tri Via*, meeting place of soldiers who, under the influence of the kind of beverage served at inns (ancient or modern), told the kind of stories and indulged in the kind of talk men usually do when they are filled with wine. Soon everybody was talking about the *Tri Via* and warning their children against the crude, cheap talk that went on at the *Tri Via*. The root of a new word, *trivial*, leaped from life into language.

Words are condensed history. Almost every word we speak has come down to us with the brains of a hundred generations distilled into it and loaded with emotional meaning. A word can excite you. A word can depress you. A word can make you sad, or glad, or mad. A page

154

full of words can destroy hope, blast a reputation, set men marching out to murder or to crusade for the truth. Words are the most powerful things on earth. "The pen," said Lytton, "is mightier than the sword." Jack London said, "The printer's ink is more intoxicating than whiskey." He was in a position to know, for he consumed a great deal of both. How many words in the dictionary? I don't know, but I can tell you there's a heap of them, all sorts of them, and they are all sound symbols of ideas.

Ann Blyth, the movie actress, made a speech on the mood of words to a distinguished gathering in Hollywood. When she finished, most of the fifteen hundred persons present asked for a copy of her talk. She said, "In the beginning was the word . . . And since then a billion, million words have been spoken. Soft words, hard words, cold words, warm words. There are words that sing and jump and skip and dance—gay words: little girl words. And words with fun in their eyes and things in their pockets and their hair mussed: little boy words. There are young words. And wise old words with a glint in their eye. There are words wide-eyed with wonder, warm, cuddly words, soft as a baby's feet. And steel words . . . stinging . . . cruel blades of words—and sweet words . . . that press their cheek against yours, [and strong father words that hold your hand and lift you up] like a child again and hoist you to their shoulders. Words are everything that man is. . . . They are his slave; they are his master—in a world at the mercy of the word of God, man is at the mercy of words."

The Christian church has an enormous stake in the treasury of words; it has almost as much stake in the dictionary as in the Bible, because words are the tools of communication, the thought conveyer of ideas. This agonizing process of finding the word, the *right* word to fit the meaning, is the enduring struggle of the church—a more urgent matter for the church than for any other institution. Consider the assignment. We are to preach the Gospel to bring the good news of God to men, to make intelligible to the world the Word of the living God; and we are to do it through the medium of words. Words are the only tools we have. We have to use the only language that we know, which is the human language, yet we are called to communicate a divine ideal, and of course it can't be done. The church has wrestled with it for nineteen centuries and has never done it. Most of the world as yet is unevangelized. We have not brought the Word of God to the world of men, principally because we are up against two almost insurmountable barriers.

First, we are up against that dumbness in the speech of men—the inadequacy of words. How can we say in words what can't be said in words? How can we dip up the ocean in a teacup, put a flower show on the radio, put the sunset glory in a sound? It can't be done. "The highest truth," Goethe said, "cannot be spoken." All great speech has pain in it because, like all great art, it is the human attempt to express the inexpressible. The artist knows the pain of that. No artist ever painted all he saw. No musician ever captured all he heard. All he can ever get is a fragment, a few stray notes, a lost chord floating down within his reach. It is part of the poet's sorrow that he can bring back from his wanderings into the infinite only little scraps of meaning.

Break, break, break,
On thy cold gray stones, O Sea!
And I would that my tongue could utter
The thoughts that arise in me.

ALFRED LORD TENNYSON

How then, can we preach the Gospel? Who hath known the mind of the Lord? People talk about the simple Gospel, the simple truth, and there is no such thing. There is only mystery on top of mystery, up into infinity, and every sermon, every poem, every scrap of writing about the ways of God, is an agonizing wrestling match with words.

A friendly postman paused at the door for a moment to chat with a little four-year-old about his baby sister. The conversation soon got around to the inevitable question concerning little girls:

"Can she talk?"

"No," the little fellow answered. "She has her teeth but her words haven't come in yet."

That is part of the pain of trying to preach—none of us has the words yet to transmit, to convey, the Word. It's what Martin Luther complained about—we preachers, when we talk about Christ, are, at best, like infants cooing and gurgling with half words and quarter words. "You must not," he said, "judge Christ by our poor efforts to describe Him." Henry Jowett said, at the end of his ministry, that the Lord we have preached about is infinitely better than all we can ever say about Him. The dumbness in the speech of men!

But that is not all that stops us. We are to preach the

157

Gospel to the world. The dumbness in the speech is matched by the deafness in the ear and a chronic dullness in the mind. To even His own disciples, Jesus said, "are ye also yet without understanding" (Matthew 15:16)? Paul preached on Mars Hill to the philosophers, the wise ones. There they sat, and he stared at them with amazement for by not one flicker of the eyelash did they evidence understanding. They just weren't getting it. They heard his words, but the insight, the meaning back of the words, was wholly lost on them. Having ears, they sat there hearing not.

We are up against that odd quirk which, in our day, has been baptized with a brand new name—semantics, the study of meanings. Two men argue about the meaning of the word and they don't understand each other because they live in different worlds. They use the same words but with meanings poles apart. Men hear not with their ears, but with their minds, their feelings, their wishes, their experiences. It is part of the barrier, they tell us, between East and West, Occident and Orient, Russia and America. We use the same words (on both sides of the iron curtain), but they don't have the same meaning. We both talk about democracy, but we don't mean the same thing. We both speak of freedom. To Americans this means freedom to choose. To others it may mean freedom from having to choose; so the words fall dead between men, or divide them through the deafness in the mind.

We need to remember that God has been up against semantics, too. The whole history of the Bible is the record of His long, agonizing struggle to reveal Himself and to break through the dullness of man's mind, through the barrier of sin and the barrier of ignorance. When God was speaking a great word about Himself, men gambled at the foot of the cross, and He prayed, "Forgive them; [they are ignorant] for they know not what they do" (Luke 23:34). It is the whole story of the Bible—a great word spoken, a great insight revealed, and always up against that dead weight of dullness. It is what Jesus put so tersely in the parable of the sower. "The seed is the word of God" (Luke 8:11), He said. The soil is the soul of man, some of it is hard soil—stony, some of it is shallow and some of it is so filled with weeds that the seed is choked before it comes to flower. God is not dumb that He should speak no more. It is the unhearing ear, the dullness in the mind.

We are wrestlers with words. Finding the word, the right word to fit the meaning, is our task. Finding the word is the enduring struggle of the church and part of the burden of God which we share in bringing His word to men. How can we get the seed into the soil? How can we reach the hearts of men with the Word of God without which they cannot live?

I want to lift up three words, three symbols of the goals toward which we must continually strive. And we're not thinking now so much of craftsmanship, techniques and methods. A minister's skill in the use of words is not the most important part of his equipment. We are thinking mostly of goals and guideposts without which we cannot preach the Word and without which we cannot reach the world. Clarity, poetry, vitality! We must make it clear: we must make it sing, and above all, we must make it live.

Clarity first. Surely we must take the great Word and make its meaning clear. At a convention on mental health, one of the speakers said that the mark of an intelligent and healthy mind is the ability to simplify the expression of an idea. It takes some doing, for it is not easy to make profound truth clear, nor to simplify the expression of an idea. I need not tell you that it is not the vogue right now. It seems rather to be the fashion, in certain sophisticated areas of artistic expression, to use symbols to conceal thought and to obscure meaning, to couch the idea in a murky vagueness intelligible only to the artistic élite. One is considered somewhat less than intellectual who aims at clarity of expression. The painting doesn't have to mean anything. The music does not need a melody. It is no business of genius to make itself explicit. Clarity is for the simpleminded. So we have painting and poetry meant to be meaningless, and when we ordinary people say we don't know what it means, our confession is taken as a compliment. The more obscure the expression, the more evident the mark of genius. When one of our top-flight poets was accused of obscurity, he said, "I can furnish ideas but I cannot furnish the brains to understand them."

Two students on their way home from a lecture walked in silence, until one said, "Wasn't that deep?" "Yep," said the other, "I couldn't understand it either."

That stratospheric aloofness is definitely not for us. We are not complaining now about the superior intellect, nor about the books beyond us that stretch the mind and make the brain perspire. We are not asking that all expression be reduced to the level of the lay mind. Doctors,

160

scientists, psychologists and theologians will have their symbols, and we must let sleeping dogmas lie.

When Bishop William A. Quayle lay paralyzed on his bed, he ordered a revised edition of the dictionary. He wanted to be sure he would recover from the correct disease.

A renowned scientist once went to Princeton to interview Albert Einstein. He had taken issue with Einstein on some phase of his unified field theory, and the two sat down in a classroom to discuss the point. I say *discuss* though neither said a word. The visitor went to the blackboard and began to write down the symbols, while Einstein sat there watching and nodding his head. For two hours, neither said a word. The visiting scientist wrote out his diagrams, symbols and equations, then rubbed them off and wrote some more. Two hours—all to disprove the theory of the shaggy headed man who watched him there in silence. Then in the third hour, when it was finished, Einstein finally spoke, "That's what you think!"

Frankly we are glad for stratospheric minds, for the men who think in those higher altitudes, where our little thoughts are lost; but the stratospheric is not for those of us whose urgent business it is to get the seed into the soil. We must wrestle with the word and make it clear, and we must simplify the expression of the idea. That takes intelligence, too. Let me illustrate.

Dr. Edmund Wylie, a Presbyterian minister, had owned the cottage which is now ours at Silver Bay, N.Y. In my study there, he told me of his friend, T. R. Glover. Glover, the renowned scholar of Cambridge, was a man with towering intellect. He knew so much about ancient Greece that someone called him Aristotle's secretary. One summer

161

while he was lecturing at Silver Bay, he was asked to preach at the Baptist Church in Hague, a small village on the edge of the Adirondack Mountains. He was perplexed as to what he would preach to a small congregation made up in part of mountain people and farmers, the opposite extreme from professional, scholarly people who were the summer visitors from the city. As he rose to speak, a flash of quiet humor was in his eye. He said, "No reputable minister would borrow another minister's sermon, but being a layman, I am more at liberty. Charles Spurgeon had a small theological school to train young men for the ministry. Part of the training was to have the student preach before the class. Mr. Spurgeon would call some young man to the front, hand him a text and ask him on the spot to preach on it. One student stood up one day and said, 'I have been given the name Zacchaeus. There are three things I would point out about Zacchaeus. I would say, in the first place, that he was a very little man, and so am I. I would remark, in the second place, that he was up a tree, and so am I. I would emphasize, in the third place, that he made haste and came down, and so will I.' As the boy took his seat, Spurgeon said, 'Young fellow, you'll get along.'

"This outline," continued Dr. Glover, "I have chosen to use today. For somewhere in the long run of life, each one of us discovers that he is a little man. It is a painful but necessary discovery. We are all like Zacchaeus—little. When we discover it, there is no help for us save that found by Zacchaeus, who climbed a tree. He sought a higher altitude. We must all do that. We must find a higher altitude that faces in the direction of the on-coming

Christ. But still there is no cure for our littleness if we let Him pass by. We can find answers for our littleness only as Zacchaeus did, who, when once he had seen Christ, made haste to come down to join His company and be part of His fellowship."

So with a wealth of illustration, some taken from the classics and *all* of them from life, the great scholar of Cambridge preached that day. Dr. Wylie said, "On my right sat a professor from Union Seminary—a scholar. On my left, a farmer who shared his hymnbook with me. When the service was over, the professor looked at me with wonder in his eyes, and said, 'Wasn't that masterful?' The horny-handed farmer put his hymnbook in the pew rack and said, 'Well, when I heerd a great professor was goin' to preach I didn't know whether I'd get anything out o' it, but I got the hull o' it. Didn't you?' "

Dr. Wylie told me that as he drove Glover back to Silver Bay he told him about it. His eyes beamed with delight. "That's a fine compliment, isn't it?" To simplify the expression of an idea—that is the mark of an intelligent mind. Clarity! We must find the word for it, wrestle with the words, sit with our head in our hands and then take the great Word and make its meaning clear.

Second—poetry! We must also make it sing. Why should the good news of God go limping along in dull and colorless prose when it was made to march to music, poetry and picture words that leap in the soul and linger to sing in the memory? Why should we leave emotion to the movies, and the vivid, colorful words to the sellers of soap, soup and refrigerators—the advertisers? Words are ignition devices, made to stir the feelings and give wings to the imagination. The real educators of this age, and of every age, are the picture makers, the storytellers —the people who remember that the common man is more emotional than rational, more a poet than a logician. He will remember a picture long after he has forgotten an argument. Shakespeare put a drop of blood on a woman's hand, and you cannot forget that picture. Churchill stood up in a day so dark the sun didn't know whether to shine or not, stuck out his British chin and, in a few vivid, colorful words, lifted a groggy nation to its feet and breathed hope into the whole free world. He could have said it in prose. "We've hard work to do, suffering to face, and we must have courage." He put it in a picture that will live as long as free men remember to be brave. "I have nothing to offer but blood, toil, tears and sweat." Try to forget it if you can!

Or try to forget the parables of Jesus—heart words, little pictures that leap in the soul and sing in the memory. He could have said it in prose. He could have said, "Don't let the world distract your praying." He said, "When thou prayest, enter into thy closet, and . . . shut thy door" (Matthew 6:6.) Common people heard Him gladly because He spoke the common speech, which is picture speech. Every peasant is a poet until he is educated beyond his native intelligence. It is a frightening thing, how dull and tame we have made the words of Christ. "His words," said Doctor E. C. Colwell, "have the . . . jagged edge of the crosscut saw. . . . His figures of speech are crammed with energy. Explosive as hand grenades, they are tossed into the crowds. . . ."

"The words," said Jesus, "that I speak unto you, they

are spirit, and they are life" (John 6:63). And if we are to speak the language of the common people, we shall have to find the heart words—words that speak to something deeper than the reason—to make men feel, and light candles in the dark. We must make the great Word clear. We must also make it sing.

Then, above all—vitality! We must make it live. No word has meaning until it comes alive. And every effort you make to find the word, the right word to say the great thing, brings you head on into the divine imperative which is the Incarnation—the Word made flesh.

Most of the great things we talk about do not exist—justice, for instance. The man on the street says, "There ain't no justice," and he is nearer the truth than we are. There *ain't* no justice. Justice is nonexistent, along with many other things we use big words for, such as freedom, truth, love, goodness, mercy. They are all abstractions. We can't even say what is meant by them until we clothe them with vitality and make them come alive.

When William James was asked to define goodness, he declined but said he could point out a good person. No word has meaning until it comes alive. In the New Testament is the story of how God came to that—the dumbness in His own speech. Through poets, prophets and holy men, for centuries and by every conceivable means, God spoke His word to men. Men heard His words but did not understand His speech, and got only a fragment of His meaning. What He wanted to say to men was beyond the power of words, until that night of nights—to use Dr. Scherer's vivid, poignantly beautiful phrase, "That night of nights when God walked down the stairs of heaven with a baby on His arm."

The Word came alive. The Word of God en-fleshed—lived, loved, dwelt among us. Through the living expression in a person we saw, we beheld His glory. It is the most wonderful story in the world—God spelling Himself out in the language of life.

I say God came to that, and when we are at this preaching business long enough, we come to it too—to the dumbness in our speech. What we are trying to say is beyond words, and must be *shown*. The divine Word must come alive in us—walk, live, love—that in the living expression through our lives the world may see the glory and the love of God.

Bishop Quayle once said that preaching is not the art of making a sermon and delivering it—preaching is the art of making a preacher and delivering that.

13

New Patches or New Creations

MATTHEW *9:14–17*

IT IS LIKELY that in His boyhood home Jesus knew something about patches. How often He had seen His mother put a patch on an old garment. How often He had worn one. And always in a poor home there comes a time when the old thing cannot be patched any more without ruining the whole thing. One day in conversation with some religious leaders, Jesus remembered that and He said, "No man putteth a piece of cloth new unto an old garment." In that small sentence He opened the door into some large issues.

I suppose the oldest controversy in history is this struggle between the old and the new, the conflict between the past and the future. It has never let up. In age after age there are patchers and creators, some who keep trying to patch up a threadbare garment and some who are forever trying to create a better new one. Where do Christians belong in this conflict? In a time of radical change, where do the followers of Christ stand? This is no longer an academic question. We have to face it now and make up our minds about it, because all our lives we shall have to live in an era of continuing unsettledness. There is no use in preparing ourselves for normal times, for we shall not have a chance to live in normal times.

The biographer of King Louis XVI said of him, "He was an amiable and upright man and doubtless would have made a good leader in times of peace." Unfortunately his ancestors had bequeathed to him a revolution. That is where we are, too; we have inherited a revolution, and we shall have to live out our days where the old and the new are clashing furiously. We carry in our own hearts the conflict that is raging without letup through the world.

David Rockefeller, when he was named Businessman of the Year, said what many others have said and in many other ways: "In [life] today the past is being overwhelmed by the future. . . . There has occurred a transformation so swift in pace and so profound in social . . . implications that it has outstripped the perception of most historians." Well, in a time of swift and profound change, where do Christians stand? What are we to be, new patches or new creations?

I believe the first thing we Christians must do in a time of radical change is to reexamine our own faith and understand as clearly as we can the progressive nature of Christianity itself. What is a Christian? I see nothing wrong with Paul's description, "If any man be in Christ, he is a new creature: old things are passed away; behold all things are become new" (II Corinthians 5:17). One of the oddest things imaginable is a Christian allergic to change when he himself is the product of the Changer, or a Christian afraid of the new when he himself has been made new. A patched coat is not a good symbol of a Christian. He may sometimes have to wear one, but he was never meant to *be* one. A Christian is a new creation in Christ with the life of the living God in him continually renewing his mind, putting off the old man and putting on the new.

The key word of the New Testament is *new*. However, could it have happened that the name of Christ in the minds of many has been linked with the forces of reaction, and that Christianity in all too many lands has been identified with old systems and institutions which have no kinship with His spirit? It is the great irony of history that the hands of Christ have been so often shackled by some of the very chains from which He came to set men free. Jesus was no patcher of old garments. He made it quite clear that this new wine, new teaching and new life was not merely a rearrangement of selfish human nature, or a patch on old material, but a new birth, a new life and a living force to create change both in the hearts of men and in the affairs of men. All these metaphors are living metaphors—seed in the earth that grows, new wine that bursts old wineskins, a vine that puts forth new branches and new fruit. The world has never realized in adequate clearness, nor have we Christian people ourselves realized, how progressive and explosive this faith of ours is: it is a living force in life that must continually dig for itself new channels and make for itself new forms. Nobody puts a new patch on an old garment. Jesus is not a patcher, He is a changer: He is the maker of new creations.

I believe we must go on to understand the processes of change, the procedures of progress and the natural laws that underlie all human advancement. They are clear enough. All progress is made by the simple technique of building in the present on some foundation of the past, taking the gains of yesterday and going further with them today. It was so obvious Jesus dismissed it with a sentence, "Think not . . . I am come to destroy, but to fulfill" (Matthew 5:17). "Ye have heard that it was said . . . of old time . . . But I say unto you" (v.21, 22). That is the key to progress in anything. That is how we build our houses: that is how we expand our business: that is how we get an education. We don't plunge in for a PhD at the age of six—at least not yet. We start in kindergarten, beginning with an alphabet and then proceeding in progressive stages to build on that and to expand our understandings of it. What a pity it is that we cannot hold to that simple procedure in the wider school of life. Here we come, all of us, tagged and labeled. We are rightists or leftists: we are conservatives or liberals. We have people who want to stay in the kindergarten and people who want to throw it out—some who want to go back to yesterday and some who just cannot wait for tomorrow. I suppose there will never be any cure for this. By temperament some of us are liberal, with our feet on the accelerator, and some are conservative, with both feet on the brakes.

A good observation has been made on this. It takes two hands to make a clock tell time. One hand goes fast and one goes slowly, and it takes both hands to make a good clock. Perhaps it takes both to make a good country or a good church. I heard Stanley Jones say once that if we were all liberal we would *blow* up, and if we were all conservative we would *dry* up. It has never been better said than by Sir Winston Churchill: "If we open a quarrel between the past and the present, we shall find that we have lost the future."

We need to understand the procedures and the underlying laws of progress. We can never get away from the past, for all our roots are in it; we dare not disregard it. The student who starts out in a chemical laboratory with contempt for the past, relying on his own originality, is likely to blow his head off before the day is out. All scientific advancement is made possible by man's experiments in the past. The New Testament is rooted in the Old. Democracy is made out of many strands woven in generations gone. America runs its roots down into many Old-World cultures, and even when we speak of the twentieth century we are acknowledging that nineteen centuries are behind us with all their history in us. If someone comes saying that Christianity is a conservative religion, he is right, if by that he means that it is profoundly grateful for the past and deeply concerned about preserving values, insights and some of the traditions which are forever true. If we ever get away from them we are lost.

We can never get away from the past, but neither can we stop there. If we see only the conservative quality in Christianity, we have not grasped the heart of it. The New Testament is not a conservative book. It is a *New* Testament. "Ye have heard that it was said . . . of old time . . . But I say . . ." We cannot stop with the old. That is what makes revolutions. Revolutions are made not alone by bad men who are out to destroy the old, but just as often by good men who refuse to grow, who want to cling to the old, to hold back and to dam up the forces which ought to flow in the normal procedures of progress. Custom—how many rivers grow stagnant in *that* swamp? How many garments have been torn on that old nail! Custom—the way we have always done it, the things we keep on doing, the words we keep on saying after life has gone out of them or leaped ahead of them!

For instance, examine the sleeve of a man's coat: there are two buttons there, or three buttons, or maybe four. There is no need for those buttons: custom put them there. We are told that in the monasteries the old monks with loose robes had trouble eating their soup, so they sewed buttons on their sleeves to keep them out of the soup. We no longer wear the robes, but we still have the buttons. We have all sorts of buttons brought over from yesterday—all sorts of things we do not need, customs we have outgrown, habits of thought grown stuffy and musty with the years.

Now let me quote a bit of verse, a little jingle with a moral.

One day, through the primeval wood
A calf walked home, as all calves should;
But made a trail all bent askew,
A crooked trail as all calves do.

Since then two hundred years have fled,
And, I infer the calf is dead,
But still he left behind his trail,
And thereby hangs my moral tale.

The trail was taken up next day
By a lone dog that passed that way;
And then a wise bell-wether sheep
Pursued the trail o'er vale and steep. . . .

And from that day, o'er hill and glade,
Through those old woods a path was made;
And many men wound in and out,
And dodged, and turned, and bent about
And uttered words of righteous wrath
Because 'twas such a crooked path.

The forest path became a lane,
That bent, and turned, and turned again;
This crooked lane became a road,
Where many a poor horse with his load
Toiled on beneath the burning sun,
And traveled some three miles in one. . . .
The years passed on in swiftness fleet,
The road became a village street;
And this, before men were aware,
A city's crowded thoroughfare;

And soon the central street was this
Of a renowned metropolis;

And o'er his crooked journey went
The traffic of a continent.
A hundred thousand men were led
By one calf near three centuries dead.
They followed still his crooked way,
And lost one hundred years a day;
For thus such reverence is lent
To well-established precedent. . . .

For men are prone to go it blind
Along the calf paths of the mind,
And work away from sun to sun
To do what other men have done.

Some of us came out of cities like that. We shall not mention any names, but there are crooked streets built on the paths of yesterday. Who wants to preserve them or patch them? Who wants to go back to the old world of high fences, greedy systems, racial egotisms, unregulated colonialisms and imperialisms? That was a crooked path. We are no more out to preserve them than the slums in our old cities. We say thank God the time is now. A voice is sounding now through all the confusion, the voice of the living, creative God, "Make [now] the crooked places straight" (Isaiah 45:2).

If we are to live as creative Christians in an age of change, we must learn to distinguish clearly between the external forms of our heritage and the inner forces that produced it. Often what puts the brake on real progress is just this: we seem more concerned about preserving the institutions that a progressive past has made than we are in reproducing in ourselves the progressive spirit that made them. That is, we want to keep what the pioneer has created, but we want to curb the pioneer spirit that creates. It is a strange mentality, and we all have it, in some degree. Think of people praising Abraham Lincoln for what he did back there but are up here denying the moral principles he stood for! Imagine people every year celebrating the revolution of 1776 but vigorously opposing any revolution going on now! That is honoring the heroes of the past whose chief honor it was that they refused to live in their past.

Jesus faced this in the Pharisees. He accused them of honoring the prophets, gilding the sepulchers of the prophets and putting flowers on the graves of the prophets; yet repeating the same sins, the same stubborn resistance to the will of God that put the prophets in their graves. Surely it should be clear that the only way we can honor the prophets is by doing in our time what they did in theirs. The only way we can honor the fathers of our country is by keeping the progressive spirit, by taking a progressive step in our time as they did in their time. It isn't necessary that we preserve all the institutions and customs they created. We honor them because that is precisely what they did not do. They broke with old customs and made new ones of their own. Consciously or unconsciously, they obeyed the principle of progress, the voice of the living God. You have heard it said of old time, but I say unto you, "Go on."

One day the disciples came to Jesus with a question, just before His ascension. They were homesick for their lost national kingdom, understandably looking back with nostalgia to the old days before Rome took over, and they said, "Wilt thou at this time restore again the kingdom to Israel" (Acts 1:7)? See? Put the old world back, restore it, change it, clean it up, but give us our old world back. It is interesting to note that Jesus did not answer that question. He transcended it. "It is not for you to know the times or the seasons . . ." He said, "But ye shall receive power . . . and ye shall be witnesses unto me both in Jerusalem . . . and unto the uttermost part of the earth" (v.8). Can you feel the force of that? It is far more important to have the power, the spirit and the vision to create new kingdoms than to restore or patch up any old kingdom that has served its day and belongs to yesterday.

In every age this story has been repeated. It is the story of people homesick for old ways, a deep reluctance in everyone to move from our seemingly solid world to the upsetness of an unknown future. There is an old and somewhat foolish story that often comes to my mind when my Scottish blood is working overtime and I get fearful, as I often do, about what is shaping up in the world. An illiterate man was walking along the old stagecoach road to Boston. All along the road, at intervals, he found slabs of stone set up. He could not read the inscriptions, but he did not want to be lacking in proper courtesy, so at every stone he would stand for a moment, take off his hat and mourn there for the unfortunate dead. Late in the afternoon a stranger met him and asked the reason for his grief. "Oh," he said, "there are so many dead along this road. Ten times I have stopped today." And the stranger said, "My friend, these are not tombstones; these are milestones. You are weeping over progress." We have all done a lot of weeping over progress. How often in history people have mourned the passing of a kingdom, the breakdown of a system, the collapse of an empire, or the changing forms in the church—gravestones which in God's good time turned out to be milestones.

No one today is weeping over the passing of monasticism, but that was sacred once. No one is weeping now over the passing of feudalism, but that was once a sacred system. No one is weeping now over the passing of the divine right of kings, but the very name betrays the sacredness with which it once was held. We are in a time again when many old things are passing away and new forces are stirring again, demanding new shapes and patterns. Of all people, we in America should be living at least as creatively as we can, for this nation itself was born out of a conflict between those who wanted to patch up an old thing and those who wanted to create a better new one. Up in Concord there is a grave which holds the bodies of five British soldiers who died on this soil in the Revolutionary War. Over it is the inscription, "They came three thousand miles . . . To keep the Past upon the throne." And not alone they; but in the colonies, too, there were loyalists who did not want to break with old ties, fearful of what might happen if they did, until some rebels met in Philadelphia and decided not to put back any old thing, but to make something new. No one today is weeping over that.

What I am pleading for is not blind belief in progress—

that is too superficial—and certainly not gullible hospitality to everything labeled new. We know that many things paraded as new are not true, and not all revolutions eventuate in progress. In fact there are many so-called new things which, as Christians, we can only deplore. The new sexual morality, for instance, is nothing but an old immorality, and most of the so-called new theology is nothing but old heresy many times discredited. There are many things labeled new on which we would like to put some brakes. What I am pleading for is a certain slant in the mind or in the heart. Call it faith, the kind of faith that runs all through the Bible—faith in the living God who is moving toward a purpose, and a response in our heart to wholeheartedly follow Him. We are not patchers of old things. We are makers of new creations.

In the old city of Haran, a legend grew up about Abraham. He was the first of that long train of spiritual pioneers striking out by faith to follow a voice, looking for a city whose builder and ruler is God. Haran was half way to the Promised Land, and on his way Abraham stopped in Haran for awhile. In his sojourn there, the legend says, he so endeared himself to the people of the place that when he felt the urge to go on they gathered around him and insisted that he remain with them and be their king. They pleaded with him; they begged him; they threatened him and finally they took him to the top of a cliff and gave him the choice of either remaining as their king or being thrust over the cliff to his death. "I have heard the voice," he said, "and I must go." So they threw him over the precipice, but Abraham landed on his feet, the legend says. And where his feet struck, two springs of fresh water sprang up. The Moslem guides today will tell you that story, and if you don't believe it, they will show you the place where his feet struck the rock, the mosque they built over it and the pool of water full of sacred fish. It is quite a tribute to Abraham that his footprints are so visible after so many years.

We are concerned about our footprints, too, and with what the future will say of us. We honor the fathers of yesterday, but we must remember that we are the fathers of tomorrow. Down there in the future, will they be able to point to some marks in the rock and say, "Here is where our fathers planted their feet: in their time they heard the voice and they obeyed, and they could not be deterred"?

14

"All the World's a Stage!"

REVELATION *1 and 4*

"AND THERE WERE great voices in heaven, saying, The kingdoms of this world are become the kingdoms of our Lord, and of His Christ; and He shall reign for ever and ever" (Revelation 11:15).

Fantastic beyond words is the vision opened by modern astronomy, telling us that these brilliant stars in the night sky, which seem like tiny lights to illuminate the earth, are not tiny lights but giant suns—great galaxies of suns, so vast and far away that their distance must be measured in light years and their number counted in the trillions. What a pitiful speck the earth is, set in the midst of unbelievable immensity! If it disappeared entirely, its removal from space would cause no more commotion than the loss of a penny from the national treasury.

The possibility of life existing in other worlds has always been fascinating. Are there people out there? Are we cousins to anybody? Are there planets like ours whirling around other suns like ours on which people live and laugh and go to church on Sunday—or stay away from church on Sunday? The subject has been debated endlessly, never so much as in our own age, the space age. And of course, nobody knows. The astronauts talk about it. The astronomers talk about it more and more, but they do not know much more about it than we do. Some are inclined to think not; at least they have examined the climatic conditions on our sister planets within our system and have come to the conclusion that the existence of life as we know it is very improbable, if not impossible. "No life anywhere," they say, "but here." If that view is right, then life hangs by a very slender thread indeed in this universe. If a million billion stars were created with only one planet where life could be, then we are back where we started before the telescope—back with the ancients who believed that this earth was the center of everything.

Apparently there are many people who vigorously take the opposite view. "We are not alone . . ." said Dr. Harlow Shapley. He speaks for many who argue that since nature seems so eager to fill even a drop of water with teeming life, it is inconceivable that multitudes of suns could exist without other planets like ours feeling a pulse of life. Dr. Shapley puts it bluntly—there are "a hundred million planetary systems suitable for organic life." It may not be life as we know it. Quite conceivably there could be other forms, other beings, different from or superior to human creatures. And so the wisest earth men cancel each other out in their speculations. We simply do not know. We only know, as Immanuel Kant said, that we are living on a little island of the known whose shores are washed by the vast waters of the unknown.

During the Second World War, a newspaperman crossed the ocean in a convoy. He said that under the cover of night a blacked-out ship was almost invisible, even to its sister ships in the convoy, but it was remarkable how the veteran seamen aboard his ship could see through that inky blackness. "A sailor stood on my left," he said, "pointed out into the darkness and said, 'You see that shape out there? That's a ship.' I could not see the end of his finger, but he could see a ship, one of our ships near enough to call to." Is that what we are here on this whirling earth, one spaceship among many ships moving in the dark within calling distance of other beings like ourselves, moving to some distant destination? Are there other people watching us as if we were a ship moving in the dark? Will these scientists sending out radio signals and hoping for an answer *get* an answer in their lifetime? Does the Almighty have other lands upon which His Spirit broods, in which His will is done? People quote Jesus and ask what He meant when He said, "In my Father's house are many mansions" (John 4:2). How the questions swarm around that one! And what did He mean by "Other sheep I have which are not of this fold" (John 10:16)? Did He mean other worlds peopled by races unlike us in our stubbornness and sin? Are we the one lost sheep of a world which the Shepherd has come to seek?

Deliberately we have started out this way to invoke an atmosphere. For that is what we need—an atmosphere, a wider vision and higher imagination—to see beyond our own little speck of a world. That is what you need when you pick up the Book of Revelation. That is what you feel as you read it—the impingement of other worlds on this one. The Book of Revelation is one of the strangest books in literature. No one understands it, including those who think they do and have it all worked out in charts and maps that show Russia to be the ten-horned beast, and the world coming to an end a year from next Friday. Maybe that sort of juggling will help you be a better Christian, but I doubt it. You must think of this Book as drama, as *great* drama, not meant to be precise but meant to make you feel something. That is what drama is: it is picture speech that describes something intensely real. Don't throw this Book out because you don't understand it. You would have to throw out almost everything on that basis. There is a profound meaning here. Milton's *Paradise Lost* and Dante's *Divine Comedy* were born in the depths of this book. Handel got both the inspiration and the words for his incomparable "Hallelujah Chorus": "He shall reign forever and ever." It is pictorial speech that means something intensely real.

John, the aged disciple, was a prisoner, exiled for his faith on the prison island of Patmos. Around him was the heaving, restless sea, and above him the pitiless glare of the sun. He spoke in visions. All great drama is born in vision. "I was in the Spirit on the Lord's day." Get into a spaceship and fly up to some point in the stratosphere from which this earth seems like a little stage across which shadows pass. From that cosmic vantage point you can see through the eyes of Him to whom a thousand years are as a day and to whom all the centuries are telescoped into hours. See from there the cavalcade of history unfold and move across the stage from creation to completion. I believe this is the atmosphere, the best mood, in which to approach the Book of Revelation.

John was writing in the first century to people who desperately needed perspective and who were going through persecution in the age of the terrible Caesars. It was a time so dangerous to be a Christian that one could not speak in simple language, but must speak in sign language, in a symbolism like that of the underground in Europe during the war. The people he was talking to could understand his imagery because they were experiencing the reality. "I was in the spirit on the Lord's Day," he said. "Write," said the voice, "the things which are, and the things which shall be hereafter." Of course, in one chapter, we cannot go into detail. All we can do is hope to give the impression that this Book leaves upon the mind and the things it makes you feel. It is precisely these convictions that bring joy in every age of time, and the first conviction is that there *is* a peopled world outside and beyond our own. "And I heard as it were the voice of a great multitude, and as the voice of many waters, and . . . mighty thunderings, saying, Alleluia, for the Lord God omnipotent reigneth" (Revelation 19:1). He reigns over other people like ourselves, yet unlike us, and over other spheres in which God moves, of which this world is a part and to which its events are related—a vast populated world surrounding this one as the ocean encircles the land.

Revelation also tells us that death is not the end of anything. Life is not a matter of life and death, but a matter of life and death and beyond it. Good and evil are not matters that are finished here but matters which in consequence reach into the hereafter.

I buried a man once who had trampled every sacred thing, broken his mother's heart and left behind him a trail of misery and sordidness. At his grave his mother stood, saying the kindest thing she could say, "Well, it's over. Thank God at last he's at rest." But I stood there thinking. Is it? Is he? "I saw the dead, small and great, stand before God; and the books were opened: . . . and the dead were judged out of those things which were written in the books" (Revelation 20:12). Another world to which this one is related exists where people live and move in continued conscious existence—this conviction is woven into all the people of the world. There is no tribe on this planet, primitive or civilized, that does not have this sense of the hereafter, however crudely the conviction is expressed. "God," said a wise man of the past, "has set eternity in the heart." And there are times when all men know that, however often the idea fades out of their minds.

A man who had served time in a state prison told how every morning the prisoners were taken out for exercise and walked a beaten path in the prison yard, around which a high wall had been erected. He said at first the impulse to see over that wall was almost torture. He could hardly resist the impulse to break out of the marching line and climb the wall, not to escape but just to see over and to look beyond the wall. As the months passed, he said he got used to it, and the impulse faded. There came a time when he walked the path and never thought of it, when he almost forgot the world beyond the wall. I wonder if you have forgotten, as you walk the path in your busyness, that the path leads through a gate and that beyond the gate is a Throne and a Book. Another world, near enough to call to!

The second impression this Book leaves in the mind is that this little world of ours has entertained a superior Visitor. A Man came to us in lowliness, walked the path with us, dwelt among us for awhile and by His words and deeds tried to make clear to us the laws of that wider Kingdom of God. He taught us that we belong to this Kingdom, that we should pray for it to come and that the will of God be done in our world as it is done in those wider spheres. He said that in the Father's house were many rooms and that love was the law that prevailed in it. He talked about eternal life, a quality of life we could come alive to, be born into, a life that is endless, that cannot die, that does not end with the earth. He tried by every conceivable means to make us see and accept that higher life.

The men of earth did not treat Him well, nor understand Him, and some did not want His truth. His light shone in the darkness and the darkness did not comprehend it and tried its best to blow it out. The world He came to was wise in many ways, but blind to the law of love. It was a bit like that primitive tribe in the old story, "The Country of the Blind." When the first civilized man came to them he told them that there were other lands beyond their little hills and other people who lived by a higher order of civilization. The people mocked him. Their leaders took counsel together, decided he was mad, and seized him and put out his eyes. So this Man with God in His eyes was a seer in the country of the blind. They did not want His kind of goodness. They strung some charges together to get rid of Him, beat Him down, spat in His face, buried Him in the earth and rolled a stone against the grave to make it as fast as they could. But the life of God was in Him, the life that cannot die, and a generation later the prisoner of Patmos said He was alive. "I am he that liveth, and was dead; and, behold, I am alive forevermore."

There are times when we perceive, too, that He is the most persistently alive Man of the ages. Again and again we have tried to bury Him, saying, "He's through, finished," but He keeps coming back. Just as we could not kill Him, neither can we kill the things in which He lives. We ride roughshod over the law of love and brotherhood only to find it coming back in some unexpected place—in dark-skinned men like Gandhi and Martin Luther King—and we are confronted again with the same problems, confronted again with a life force that can never be stopped or exhausted. His coming into history marked an epoch in it, split it in two, for He introduced a new vitality in which the life force shot up higher, as it did when light first came to be. John tells us that He's alive in the world: he never lets us forget that.

The third unforgettable impression the Book leaves upon the mind is that of the final triumph of His kind of goodness and the doom of all human ways that reject it. Take your place with John on his star up there and see the curtain rise and fall on its history. "After this I looked," he said. And a voice said, "Come up hither, and I will shew thee things which must be hereafter." And behold a throne was set in heaven—a throne. Nearly fifty times in the Book John talks about that throne—symbol of the ultimate center—the Divine authority before which all men and nations are judged and must ultimately bend the knee. A throne was set in heaven.

Then like a mighty drama you see the vision begin to unfold. In moving pageantry with a kaleidoscopic shifting of scenery, the cavalcade of the ages is written out. One after another the great world empires pass in review, play their little parts on the stage and pass into history: each is pictured as a beast symbolizing its kind of power, and the glory of them all is judged by the authority of the throne.

There are some people who think they understand what all these weird symbols mean. Maybe so. Frankly, I do not, and since those who assume they do sharply disagree with each other, I propose to wait for wiser interpreters. But as to the message behind the imagery there need be no confusion. What we have here is a description in highly symbolic language of a warfare that is intensely real— the agelong conflict between flesh and spirit, darkness and light, Babylon and the new Jerusalem, the city of man and the City of God, the kingdoms of this world and the kingdoms of the living God. It is a story of strife and struggle, of victory and defeat, in which truth seems forever on the scaffold and wrong forever on the throne; but the scaffold sways the future, and behind the dim unknown standeth God.

The Apostle Paul stands before Nero, the monster-man. Nero condemns righteous Paul to death. It takes a long time in history until people begin calling their sons Paul and their dogs Nero, but as sure as there is a throne, that time comes. You sense this all through the revelation —the ultimate, inescapable authority of the throne.

There are some people repelled by the language of the Book. Some have said it should never have been put in the Bible as Christian literature because its military, bestial symbols are offensive and fantastic to the Christian mind. Maybe so, but they were not fantastic in the world of that day. That was a bestial age. That was a cruel time between the fire of Rome and the fall of Jerusalem. John was simply writing down what he saw. He saw the Rome of the Caesars try to snuff out the church and the synagogue. He saw the kingdoms of this world try to beat down the little kingdoms of truth, springing up here and there. He saw a great materialistic system rise up: he called it Babylon, Mother of Abominations, drunk with the wine of kings and the blood of martyrs. He talks about bowls of wrath poured out, about nations like snarling beasts rising out of the sea, about birds of prey swooping down on their victims, dragons lifting up their horny heads and the four horses of the apocalypse riding roughshod over men, bringing war, famine, disease and revolution, while messengers of mercy wing their way from heaven to earth and back again.

Of course that is fantastic, but what about the reality it describes? The world was like that: nations were like snarling beasts pouncing on each other in the mad struggle for world power. I wonder how ancient it is. What about our own history? Will not the history of the future, looking back over our century—the bloodiest century in history—have to write it in terms of military, bestial language? Indeed, what are the symbols of big nations today? We are trying to reach a peace table somewhere.

Around it will hover at least four great powers—Russia, China, Britain and America. What are the symbols of these nations? Russia, the great bear with its huge fore-paws; Britain, the lion, most ferocious of all beasts; China, the dragon waking out of sleep, terrible in its might; America, the eagle with its talons, swooping on its foe. The old standards of the Roman legion! These are not symbols the Bible has given us: they are symbols the nations themselves have chosen to express the spirit of their people. Nations are like football teams. They choose names to strike terror into the enemy—Wolverines, Wildcats, Gators, Rams, Bulldogs, and we try to get peace with that spirit. We bring bears and lions and dragons and eagles around a peace table. How do you get peace out of a menagerie like that?

John was writing what he saw. The Bible is more realistic about human nature than we are, with our naive optimism, about the innate goodness of man. The world of man is beastly still. Human nature without God is monstrous. The heart of man is still wild, untamed and unredeemed. We are learning that again, in the upsurge of violence now shaking the earth, whether it is black power burning shops in the slums or white power burning two hundred Negro churches, shooting good men in the back or standing by glad that it is done. We are learning again, though our fathers knew it well, that down underneath the veneer of civilization there still lurks the old savagery of the primitive man, which, if unchecked, might tear the fabric of civilization to pieces.

John was writing what he saw. He put it down faithfully: he made no attempt to twist the truth or shut his eyes to the dark facts about the kingdoms of this world. He was not afraid to face the problem because he knew the answer. The answer is in the throne and in the spirit of Him who reigns from it, King of Kings, Lord of Lords, before whose moral brightness the terrors are vanquished and evil slinks away into the darkness. The lie cannot live in His presence. It beats its head against the throne.

There is great hope in the fact that something is here that will not let evil come right. Evil cannot win anything or build anything in the long pull. All it can do is to bark its shins against defeat and stumble in the darkness toward the light of God—which is exactly what it *is* doing. There is a throne.

And that is why we need the Easter message, not to prove there is a heaven hereafter to which nice people go when they die; but to remind us, in the struggles of a discouraging time, that there is a throne, there is a Book and there is a moral warfare in which we must take sides. I heard great voices in heaven saying, "The Lord God omnipotent reigneth." And the hope is that more and more great voices on earth are now seeing and saying it, too: "There is a Throne."

Do you remember the story of Queen Victoria, when Handel's *Messiah* was first played in England in a large hall and in the Queen's honor? It had already become the custom for people on the Continent to rise to their feet at the "Hallelujah Chorus," but everyone thought the Queen should remain seated by reason of her station. Yet when the great strains of majestic music floated out, "And He shall reign for ever and ever. He shall reign for ever

190

and ever," the Queen with fine insight got to her feet, lifted the crown from her head and stood with bowed head with the rest, a prophecy of that day when every eye shall see and every tongue confess, and the kingdoms of this earth have been made the kingdoms of Him whose throne is set forever in the heavens and in the little earth.